dare to be square quilting

dare to be square quilting

A Block-by-Block Guide to Making Patchwork and Quilts

BOO DAVIS

POTTER
CRAFT

NEW YORK

dedication

To Heather, Michele, and Whitney. What would I do without my girlfriends?

Copyright © 2010 by Boo Davis

Published in the United States by Potter Craft, an imprint of the Crown Publishing Group, a division of Random House, Inc., New York. www.crownpublishing.com www.pottercraft.com

POTTER CRAFT and colophon is a registered trademark of Random House, Inc.

Library of Congress Cataloging-in-Publication Data
Davis, Boo.
Dare to be Square Quilting: A Block-by-Block Guide to making patchwork and quilts/
by Boo Davis ; photographs by Jennifer Levy ;
illustrations by Boo Davis.
p. cm.
Includes index.
ISBN 978-0-307-46236-7
1. Patchwork—Patterns. 2. Quilting—Patterns. 3. Square in art. I. Title.
TT835.D3728 2010
746.46'041—dc22
2009040525

Printed in China

Art direction by Chi Ling Moy
Design by 3&Co.
Photography by Jennifer Lévy
Step-by-step photos by Chris Larralde
Illustrations by Boo Davis
Photography pages 10 and 36 by Aaron Kaffen
Photography page 13 by Dindy Yokel
Grateful acknowledgment is made to Jesse LeDoux.

10 9 8 7 6 5 4 3 2 1

First Edition

contents

introduction

The strange patchwork-brick road that led from Ozzy Osbourne to this book began in my childhood bedroom. There, I spent my awkward teen years listening to the classics—Black Sabbath, Iron Maiden, and Metallica—beneath my grandmother's quilt. I could have taken refuge under that quilt forever, lost in "Diary of a Madman" and exploring the terrain of Grandma's patchwork. Hours flew by as I pondered fabric choices, delighted in color tensions, and considered the love behind every misaligned seam and crooked stitch. That simple pink and green yarn-tied quilt sparked my obsession with patchwork.

But it wasn't until college that I joined the ranks of self-taught quilters. My launch into quilt-making began with hand-piecing nine-patch squares with a friend on snowy, miserable nights at Northwestern University. I obsessively read quilting books when I should have been revising my journalism homework. To beef up my fabric stash, I spent weekends getting lost on bike rides to quilting shops that were three towns over. My dorm-mates would inquire about my "square" new hobby: "Why quilting? Why not pickling or jam-making?" After college, I took quilting classes and made the leap to a sewing machine. That's when the fabric really hit the fan.

After making what seemed like the hundredth blanket for a friend's newborn, I had an epiphany: Why not an evil, heavy metal quilt made just for me? It seemed perfectly natural that my two great loves—quilting and heavy metal music—could work together in some sort of unholy alliance. That's when Quiltsrÿche, my one-woman quilt sweatshop, was born. My mission statement: "Making modern heirloom quilts just like your metal-loving, half-blind grandma would." I transformed traditional log cabin patterns into skulls. I manipulated Roman stripes into the iconic "devil's horns" hand gesture. I set out to reinterpret quilt traditions in a hard-edged—but heartfelt—new way.

When presented with the challenge of making a beginner's guide to quilting, I had to push beyond patchwork Grim Reapers and Flying V guitars. Let's face it, a fun and approachable introduction to quilting probably doesn't include a "Gates of Hell" quilt for most of you. So I rethreaded my formula: more cute, less evil. Luckily, the transition from sinister to sweet was a seamless one. Even without the heavy metal edge, this book is still infused with Quiltsrÿche's brand of heart, humor, and graphic boldness. Who knew I'd love owls and robots just as much as I love bats and amplifiers?

My approach to quilting is an approach for true beginners. I don't like triangles, circles, hexagons, diamonds, rhombuses, or any shape that makes measuring a chore. (Can we stop right here and ponder *rhombus*? Man, that word is hilarious.) In this book, every project is designed using only squares and rectangles. Why just squares and rectangles? Because straight seams are easy to stitch! Plus, squares and rectangles don't require fussy templates to cut out, just simple math and use of a grid. You'll be amazed at what bold and exciting quilt designs can be achieved using only straight-sided shapes with right-angled corners.

I'm not going to lie to you. Quilting can be time-consuming, arduous, and best left to the OCD types. Quilts aren't make-'em-in-a-weekend craft projects; they are labor-intensive, usable pieces of art that can be handed down for generations. But if you are a weekend warrior, I've got you covered with the eye-popping patchwork projects in Part 3 of this book. These crafty items offer all the satisfaction of patchwork without the time commitment of a full-size quilt.

Because time is valuable, you can be sure the techniques I'm presenting here are the fastest, easiest, and most reliable methods that modern quilting has to offer. Techniques like rotary cutting, chain-piecing, machine-quilting, and machine-binding can help you avoid Quilting Burnout and move you along to your next project with your sanity intact. Life's too short for methods that take ten times as long only to look 10 percent better.

Not only do you have permission to take a few shortcuts, you also have full permission to make mistakes. Embrace goof-ups like misaligned seams, wobbly stitching, and bunching. Err on the side of the unusual with overlooked fabrics and oddball color combinations. A quilt should be as complex and perfectly imperfect as you. I promise that your sewing skills and quilting confidence will develop quickly, but in the meantime, these quilts and projects are so fun and forgiving, they'll look fantastic any way you stitch them. So relax and enjoy the quilt-making process. Dare to make a quilt that's funny, fabulous, and from the heart . . .

Dare to be square!

PART 1:
Patchwork and Quilting Basics

This section is like Quilting 101: It will arm you with enough information to tackle every project in this book. The first step to becoming a powerhouse of patchwork and a crusader of quilt-making is understanding these basic terms. What exactly *is* patchwork? And can something be *both* patchwork *and* a quilt? Yes it can! **Patchwork** describes any design pieced together from shapes of fabric, such as squares and rectangles. When used to make a **quilt,** patchwork becomes the top of a quilt's three layers, sitting above a fluffy middle layer of batting and a bottom layer of backing. These layers are held together by **quilting**, either by hand or machine using a straight stitch, or instead of quilting, the layers are tied together at regular intervals with yarn. Making a patchwork quilt doesn't require any special skills, just some general sewing know-how and the nerve to try it!

To make the patchwork and quilt projects in this book, you'll be using techniques that are the fastest, easiest, and most reliable methods out there. As you read these instructions on basic cutting, piecing, quilting, and binding methods, you'll also find tips on selecting fabric and a primer on my **"scraphazard"** approach to quilt design. You're about to see how fresh, interesting quilts get made when *scrappy* and *haphazard* collide. Every technique you'll learn here calls for 100 percent machine construction—which is a bit too nontraditional for some. But not you! You want to make exciting, personality-packed quilts quickly and easily. My hope is that you'll look at quilt-making a bit differently, and make the process work better for you. And, most important, you'll have fun!

patchwork and quilting basics

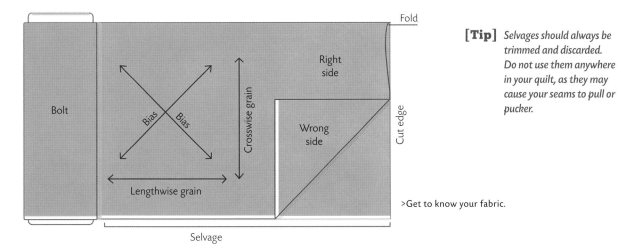

Fold

Right side

Crosswise grain

Bolt

Bias Bias

Cut edge

Wrong side

Lengthwise grain

Selvage

[Tip] *Selvages should always be trimmed and discarded. Do not use them anywhere in your quilt, as they may cause your seams to pull or pucker.*

>Get to know your fabric.

materials

The anatomy of a quilt begins and ends with fabric, the most important and fun material for most quilters. However, the choices you make for thread and batting are equally important. Think about your project's indestructibility over the long haul when choosing materials. Your quilt's life expectancy is equal to the durability of the lowest-quality material or most worn piece of fabric in your patchwork. And whether it's fabric, thread, or batting—cotton is king!

FABRIC

Make an heirloom-quality quilt—the kind you'll pass down to your grandkids' grandkids—by using 100 percent cotton fabric of the caliber sold at specialty quilting shops. High-quality quilting cotton lasts longer, wears better, and is easier to work with than any other material. While quilt shops are failsafe, go-to locales for supremely soft, high-thread-count, 100 percent cotton, you can train yourself to recognize suitable fabric anywhere.

Quality quilting cottons have higher thread counts—around 70 threads per square inch of fabric. Because manufacturers don't include this information on the bolt, you have to "eyeball" the fabric. Check the density of the fabric's weave by holding it up to the light. Does the fabric have a loose weave you can see right through? Does it feel thin and limp? Or is it heavily starched and chemical-

smelling? If you answered "yes" to any of these questions, drop that fabric and move on.

[Tip] *Hey, quilt genius! You'll find important terms in boldface throughout this section defined in the glossary on page 156.*

Vintage fabric will add loads of character to your quilt—just make sure it's really cotton and not a polyester imposter. To tell if polyester has infiltrated your fabric, fold it onto itself and run it between your fingers. Is it slippery? Does it hold a crease? A true cotton has a bit of grip to it and holds a sharp crease. When in doubt about a fabric's fiber content or thread count, leave it out of your quilt design.

Before you start using any fabric, wash it in warm water with a gentle soap and machine-dry. Remove the fabric from the dryer while it's still damp and promptly iron. Prewashing prevents disasters like shrinkage and bleeding in a finished project. To avoid a tangled ball of unraveled threads in the washer, trim the cut edges of your fabric with pinking shears prior to washing. I suggest making a habit of prewashing all of your fabric conquests right when you bring them home.

As you evaluate fabrics, you'll notice that most have a **right side**, on which the pattern is printed, and a **wrong side**. You'll also find that although fabric is manufactured in various widths, the most common width for cotton quilting fabric is 45". This width includes the **selvage**, which forms the tightly woven finished edge of the fabric. Keeping your

THREAD

Choosing thread for your quilt may not be as much fun as choosing fabric, but it is no less important. After all, you want those seams to stay where you put them! The common practice among quilters is to match the thread fiber to the fabric—when using good-quality, 100 percent cotton fabric, use good-quality, 100 percent cotton thread. The theory is that cotton thread and cotton fabric are equal in strength and therefore wear evenly. A good-quality thread is smooth and durable, gives you well-defined stitches, and doesn't leave excessive fuzz behind on your sewing machine. When shopping the thread aisle at your local sewing shop, look for all-purpose cotton thread for general machine sewing. Ask a salesperson to recommend a trusted brand of thread. As for my preference, I love Mettler threads because of their durability and wide range of colors.

A neutral-colored thread in gray or beige works best for **piecing** together the fabric in your quilt top. These neutrals tend to blend with the patchwork and will be less visible to

eye on the selvage is fundamental to quilt-making. You'll use it to help you square up the fabric before cutting by identifying the direction of the **grain** lines.

To make your quilt fit together accurately, it's important to cut and sew "on grain." If you don't, your fabric may stretch, distort, and create headaches for you every step of the way. The **lengthwise grain** of fabric runs parallel to the selvages and has little stretch. It's the strongest grain in your fabric, so long pieces of patchwork should be cut to run parallel to this grain. The **crosswise grain** runs perpendicular to the selvages and has a slight stretch. The **bias** runs at a 45-degree angle to selvages and has maximum stretch, which distorts easily. Never cut on the bias for the straight-sided projects in this book.

>Quilt-making in Gee's Bend (sidebar). Mary Lee Bendolph's quilts air-drying outside her Alabama home.

the eye. The color of thread for the actual quilting stitches is a personal design choice—if you want your quilting to stand out, use a contrasting thread color. I love utilitarian off-white thread that looks straightforward and clean—no matter what colors predominate in my quilt top. But, when finishing the raw edges of a quilt with a thin strip of binding fabric, I prefer to match the thread to the binding, to not draw any attention to it. This is where a wide selection of thread colors comes in handy!

BATTING

Batting is the fluffy, warm middle layer of your quilt. It comes in different "lofts" (or thicknesses) and fibers, including cotton, polyester, cotton/poly blends, wool, and even bamboo. Low-loft 100 percent cotton batting is the choice of most serious quilters because it's durable, breathable, and machine-quilts beautifully. Most natural fiber battings are low- to mid-loft, while polyester batting can achieve high-loft fluffiness. I use the brands Warm & Natural and Warm & White, because I enjoy their softness, density, and traditional flat look—but there are several reliable manufacturers of 100 percent cotton batting on the market. If in doubt, ask a salesperson for her recommendation.

Use what ya got!

Quilt-making was once regarded as a thrifty way to use up scraps of fabric. Clever quilt-makers from days of yore eked out every last bit of usefulness from textile fragments, creating stunning works of art for everyday use. Nobody embodies this scrappy spirit more than the quilt-makers of Gee's Bend, Alabama. Working with limited access to fabric in a poor and isolated community, for generations these women transformed old work clothes, dresses, feed sacks—anything they could get their hands on—into boldly composed works of quilted art. Today, the quilters of Gee's Bend are considered artists in their own right, but they still employ the same methods and techniques learned from their forebears. I salute this sort of resourcefulness! Try using the Gee's Bend improvisational design approach and "use what ya got" fabric strategy. Challenge yourself to keep your wallet shut and use just the fabric you have on hand. Go to your fabric stash, pick out a print you overlooked before, and pair it with something in a truly unexpected way. Try using the wrong side of a fabric—you may prefer its lighter values! Or perhaps now is the time to coordinate a fabric swap with your crafty friends. Working within fabric limitations just might lead to a design breakthrough!

Batting comes either precut in mattress sizes or by the yard. (Refer to Choosing a Quilt Size, page 20, for mattress size information.) The precut sizes usually accommodate the extra 5" in length and width of batting you need when assembling your quilt. Use bleached white cotton batting if you have bright or white colors in your quilt to give them extra vibrancy. Otherwise, choose the unbleached kind. Organic cotton? Even better.

Unlike fabric, there's no need to prewash your batting; in fact, its slight shrinkage in your finished quilt creates old-fashioned texture and accentuates the quilting. If you do choose to prewash, read the manufacturer's recommendations. Also, note the manufacturer's suggested "quilting intervals"—some batting requires you to stitch your projects at close distances (like every 2" or 3") to prevent the batting from shifting and lumping up between quilting lines.

essential tools and equipment

On the following pages you'll find a list of my go-to tools, which I consider essential for quilting. If you've ever attempted to sew on a button or hem some pants, you're probably in possession of several sewing basics already. As you acquire tools for your new favorite hobby, buy the best you can afford, borrow what you can, or make do until you can upgrade. I prefer a minimalist approach, but it's easy to be suckered by the hundreds of specialty tools that make quilting tasks easier or more accurate. When you feel overwhelmed by the options out there, remember that quilters throughout the eons have made amazing works of art with subpar equipment and limited resources.

SEWING MACHINE & ACCESSORIES

Sewing machine: For years I made quilts on an inexpensive entry-level sewing machine I named "Donkey" because it was loud and bucked with each stitch. Now I use a machine designed specifically for quilting, with features intuitive to patchwork and quilting tasks. But it's not about

the sewing machine—it's about the user! You can make exceptional quilts on whatever machine you have. All you need a machine to do is sew straight seams, backstitch, and set different stitch lengths. All you'll need to learn are the basic functions of the machine and how to adjust the tension to keep stitches even and consistent. For best results, keep the owner's manual within reach at all times.

¼" Quilting foot: One of the most convenient machine accessories for quilters is a ¼" quilting foot. This makes piecing a no-brainer because you simply align the edge of your fabric with the edge of your **presser foot** to get accurate ¼" seams. Try to buy a quilting foot made by your sewing machine's manufacturer. If you can't find one, you can purchase a generic foot. Ⓐ

Walking foot: Use a walking foot to evenly guide all three layers of the quilt—top, batting, and backing—through your machine. I've quilted many projects without a walking foot, but this attachment helps reduce the frustration of layers shifting out of alignment. See if your machine's manufacturer offers a walking foot. Otherwise, buy a universal version. Ⓑ

Machine needles: Always keep a fresh supply of needles on hand, and replace your sewing needle at the start of each big project. Sizes 75/11 and 80/12 of the "sharp" type will see you through the entire quilt-making process. Ⓒ

Seam ripper: This simple tool is an absolute necessity in quilting. Keep this handy for removing machine-sewn stitches and quickly putting any mistakes in the past. Ⓓ

MEASURING, MARKING, & CUTTING

Rotary cutter: A rotary cutter looks like a pizza cutter. But instead of dough, this tool cuts strips, straightens fabric edges, and produces multiple geometric pieces at lightning speed. A good first blade is the 45mm, but a big fat 60mm is my weapon of choice. Change the blade on your rotary cutter every few projects. Ⓔ

Rotary cutting mat: A rotary cutting mat will be your home base for much of the quilt-making process. Don't cheap out by purchasing a smaller mat. Trust me, you'll just end up buying the big daddy sooner or later. Only the big 24" x 36" mat can accommodate cutting long strips of standard 45"-wide quilting fabric from selvage to selvage (that is, when the fabric is folded in half lengthwise, with the selvages on top of each other). Ⓕ

Ruler: An acrylic ruler provides the edge that guides the rotary cutter and is marked with lines to aid in measuring. A 6" x 24" will be your go-to ruler because it's long enough to cut standard 45"-wide quilting fabric from selvage to selvage. Ⓖ

Scissors: Big and small pairs of scissors are crucial to any quilting setup. Tiny embroidery scissors are convenient for cutting threads, while a larger set of dressmaking shears will be useful for a surprising number of tasks. A pair of pinking shears is handy for trimming off the cut edges off fabric prior to prewashing, preventing a tangled ball of thread that can develop in the washer. Ⓗ

Tape measure: A tape measure is good to have on hand. Since we're not measuring around curves, a contractor-style metal one works best. Ⓘ

Quilt pencils: These fabric-marking pencils wash out easily and are great for marking fabric pieces with pattern letters to avoid confusion. Keep a variety of colors on hand to mark both light- and dark-colored fabrics. Ⓙ

PINS & NEEDLES

Straight pins: These pins keep your fabric from shifting as you work. For patchwork, very thin pins are best, since they won't leave marks on your fabric. Ⓚ

Curved quilting needles: These needles are terrific for thread **basting** (that's when you temporarily secure all of the layers of your quilt together with thread before quilting) because they are less challenging to pull through flat fabric layers than regular straight needles. Ⓛ

Bent-arm safety pins: Special bent-arm safety pins are perfect for quickly basting smaller projects. Ⓜ

Pincushion: In my opinion, a magnetic pincushion is the only way to go. I have a couple positioned at different workstations in my quilt studio. The flat, magnetized surface is an easy target to hit when you're pulling pins with one hand and wrangling fabric through a machine with the other. Ⓝ

PRESSING NEEDS

Iron and ironing board: A steam iron is essential for pressing wrinkle-free cotton fabric and making your patchwork flat and crisp. Keep the iron and ironing board setup close to your workstation.

Where to find materials and tools

Specialty quilting shops are the most reliable source of specialized tools and quilter-approved materials. When shopping the designated quilting sections at large chain or discount fabric stores, be choosy about fabric quality, because most often you get what you pay for. However, mass-market fabric stores can be great places to stock up on solid fabrics from reliable manufacturers, like Kona Cotton by Robert Kaufman, and on basic sewing supplies. Most mega stores have frequent sales, so proper planning may land you big savings on your quilting start-up costs. Shopping online will often yield web-only deals year-round.

Make a habit of browsing Craigslist and eBay for quilting fabric and tools. You'll often stumble upon someone cleaning out craft room and unloading her fabric stash by the pound. Estate sales can occasionally yield a fabric wonderland. You'd be amazed at what crafty people with fabric-hoarding streaks will leave behind. Load up on fabric at low prices (like 50 cents a yard)—just check for quality before you lay down your hard-earned change.

Spray bottle: Several spritzes of water from a spray bottle works better than an iron's built-in steam function for getting out truly stubborn wrinkles.

QUILTING & BINDING TOOLS

Painter's tape: Use painter's tape to secure the layers of your quilt while basting, and as a guide for straight-line quilting. Painter's tape is less sticky than masking tape and comes in widths of 1½", 2", and 3". ◎

Wood molding: An inexpensive piece of 6'-long wood molding, when used with painter's tape, is a terrific (but optional) tool in marking straight quilting lines on your quilt. The wood molding provides a stable, straight edge to run a strip of tape alongside, preventing the tape from bowing across a long distance. You can find this item at your local home-improvement store.

Binding tape maker: Tape makers quickly fold the raw edges of a fabric strip toward its center, producing perfectly folded binding that can be easily sewn over a quilt's raw edges. Get the 1" tape maker that accommodates 2" strips. Ⓟ

[Tip] *Keep several lint rollers on hand to tame the constant barrage of stray threads and miscellaneous fuzzy debris that collects on your projects.*

designing your quilt

Here's where we get to the fun stuff. Designing is the most exhilarating and creative part of quilt-making. If your color and fabric choices are duds, not even perfect craftsmanship will save your project. Fortunately, there are some useful guidelines for choosing colors and fabrics that work together—whether they are solid colors or crazy prints, brand-new or vintage. To make a quilt with distinct personality and true scrap appeal, tune your radar to the lovely, unassuming fabrics that don't really know they're cool.

Not that you shouldn't use the fabulous print in that hip fabric shop's window—just don't rely on all of its coordinating fabrics that have been conveniently preselected for you. Your personality gets pushed aside when you let too many popular prints produced by lifestyle experts take center stage. So do things the hard way: Amass modest fabrics you love little by little. Let them look imperfect bouncing off one another. Your quilt should tell *your* story, not showcase your ability to buy designer.

FABRIC CASTING CALL:
Combining fabrics

A successful quilt features proper proportions of three types of fabrics: solids, supporting prints, and star players. This mix gives your quilt texture, movement, and scrappy panache. Quilt queen Denyse Schmidt recommends a mix of 30 percent prints to 70 percent solids. I think that's a great proportion to shoot for, but each quilt is different, so don't be afraid to listen to your own intuition as you experiment with fabric.

Solids: Solids are the unsung heroes of good quilt design and should predominate in your project. These powerful yet unpretentious beauties keep the design humming, create calm amidst chaos, and give your design sharp definition. I like to choose unpredictable color combinations that give a jolt to the viewer. Quirky color inspiration is all around you—start taking note! Purchase solids from several different manufacturers to get a nice variation of colors in your fabric stash.

[Tip] *Repeat success. If you find a combination of fabrics that play well together, repeat the winning team in other places around the quilt.*

Supporting prints: It's these modest prints that help bridge the gap between solids and star players. They do the heavy lifting and are usually responsible for holding designs together. Simple stripes, polka dots, plaids, calicoes, and checks add vitality and movement while providing visual relief from busy prints. These versatile team-players should be the "go-to" prints on your fabric roster.

Star players: These personality-packed prints are high maintenance and should be used sparingly. Often playing the role of "inspiration fabric," these attention-getters can be swirling all-over patterns, florals, or bold geometric designs. While visually arresting and seductive, a quilt with too many can exhaust the eye. Surround these fabrics with an entourage of supporting prints and solids so their individuality can be appreciated.

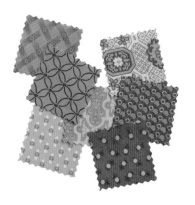

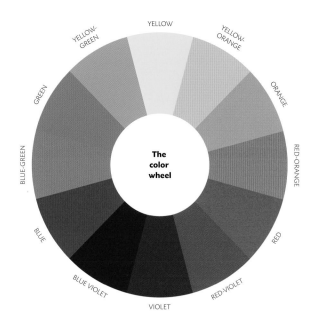

THERE ARE NO BAD COLOR COMBINATIONS:
Using a color wheel

Throw out those rules about what colors do or don't go together—you can make any color combination work by playing with variations of it. You just need some color wheel know-how! While this handy tool can't make color decisions for you, it can help you understand the relationship between colors—and that makes choosing fabric a bit easier.

The basic color wheel arranges twelve distinct, pure colors in a circle. Every other color we see is a variation created by tweaking these twelve distinct colors—mixing them to create new hues, adding black to create darker *shades*, adding white to make lighter *tints*, and adding gray to alter their intensities, making *tones*.

As you examine the color wheel, you'll notice that each color blends into the next. Colors that sit beside each other look great together naturally because their color DNA is similar. These neighboring colors are called **analogous** and feel harmonious and soothing as combinations. A simple color strategy in quilt design is choosing an inspiration color from the wheel, then adding hits of analogous color from each side of it.

Juxtaposin':
Show us your contrast

Amping up the contrast in your quilt will make it a vibrant success instead of a washed-out flop. To create memorable effects in your patchwork, use fabrics that contrast with one another both in value and scale. But beware of too much contrast within any single fabric—this can throw your entire design out of whack.

Mix light, medium, and dark values. Value is the degree of lightness or darkness of a color and is almost more important to the success of a design than color itself! Choose a range of light, medium, and dark fabrics to give your quilt depth and interest. If you'd like some reassurance that your fabric choices contain a good range of values, you can buy a nifty tool at a quilt shop called a "value finder." This is a small rectangle made of transparent red plastic that, when held over fabrics, allows you to see their true value without the distraction of color and prints.

Combine small, medium, and large-scale prints. Using patterned fabric adds a traditional feel to your projects—after all, they are the hallmark of quilt-making! For best results, use a combination of small-, medium-, and large-scale prints. Strive for a mix of widely spaced motifs and more compact designs. Small-scale prints provide a valuable service because they look solid from a distance but add a little something special up close.

Choose low- to medium-contrast prints. Contrast within a quilt design may be the goal, but contrast within a fabric is another story. Choose prints that have low to medium contrast only—they are the most versatile and will be easy to mix and match. You're going to find that **monochromatic** (one color) prints are especially hardworking in your designs. Avoid high-contrast prints—they are serious divas that command center stage and don't play well with others. Be wary of white in a print because it usually ups the contrast level dramatically, making a fabric difficult to work into a design.

Want some pop in your color choices? Choose colors directly opposite on the color wheel. Called **complements**, these colors stand out against each other and create visual tension. For example, a predominantly blue quilt would get a big jolt of energy when fabrics with complementary orange are added to the design.

So which colors win in a battle of color dominance? **Dominant colors** are the first colors you see when looking at a quilt. Using blue and orange again as an example, orange would beat out blue in dominance, because of its *temperature*. Warm colors, such as orange, on the right side of the color wheel, are more dominant and will advance in your quilt. Cool colors, on the left side of the color wheel, recede and fade into the background a bit. You can control which parts of a quilt pattern advance or recede, depending on the fabrics you choose. Colors advance when they are warm, dark, or pure. Colors recede when they are cool, light, or toned down with gray. Color dominance can be tricky—you can follow these general guidelines, but ultimately it will depend on the proportion and distribution of fabrics in a design.

Choosing a quilt size

The quilts in this book are sized at approximately 60" x 72"—slightly smaller than a store-bought quilt sized for a twin bed. However, this is a size that's realistic for beginners to quilt on their home sewing machines without frustration. It's also the perfect size to use around the house—whether it's a throw for your bed or for the couch. If you'd like a larger quilt, follow the suggestions accompanying each project on how to expand the pattern. Always make sure to sketch your resized quilt on paper to see how the change in scale will affect the design.

	Standard mattress size	With a 12" drop on three sides
Twin	39" x 75"	63" x 87"
Double	54" x 75"	78" x 87"
Queen	60" x 80"	84" x 92"
King	76" x 80"	100" x 92"

SCRAPHAZARD QUILT DESIGN:
Using a design wall

Few things are as charming as a seemingly effortless, random smattering of prints in a quilt. These quilts have a "scraphazard" beauty that invites you to admire their patchwork for hours—and still discover new bits of fabric. You can create a one-of-a-kind quilt with true scrap appeal with the help of a design wall. This space gives you an overall vertical view of your quilt-in-progress and lets you move fabric pieces around at your whim. It's nearly effortless to swap a bold floral for a demure Swiss dot—then stand back and take it all in. Give it a try and unleash your inner collage artiste. Just hang a large piece of flannel or low-loft batting on a wall and start adding fabrics in whatever combination you like. Cotton quilting fabric magically adheres to the nubby flannel, so there's no need for pins. I've used the same inexpensive, flannel-backed plastic tablecloth for years to create a design wall; as a bonus, this "wall" can be rolled up and transported in mid-design!

Here's how to create a quilt with scraphazard charm that's all your own:

1. **Lay a solid foundation.** First, lay out your quilt using only solid fabrics. Using your rotary cutter, ruler, and mat, cut out pieces of pre-washed solid fabric according to the cutting guide that accompanies your project. (Refer to page 22 for instructions on cutting fabric.) Position each piece on your design wall as indicated by the pattern diagram. A solids-only foundation provides a baseline to build upon—or fall back on if your fabric choices should take a wrong turn. A solids-only layer also eliminates the anxiety of a completely blank canvas and frees you to be adventurous!

[Tip] *Take digital photos as you work. Photos will document your process and provide a record of successful fabric configurations to fall back on if you veer off course. It's as close as you can get to an "undo" button.*

> Before: Lay a solids-only foundation.

> During: Swap in different prints.

> After: The final scraphazard masterpiece.

2. **Swap in different prints.** Select a stack of printed fabrics you think might work in your quilt. Replace several solid fabric pieces with print pieces in the corresponding color. Layer print pieces directly on top of the solids—they'll stick! Treat your quilt like a collage, and try out a mix of prints by cutting out pieces one by one, swapping them in and out until you've reached a lively balance of plain and patterned. A mix of 30 percent prints and 70 percent solids is a good goal, but trust your design instincts. You'll end up with a stack of unused solid pieces. Worry not! You'll use them in future projects.

[Tip] *Employ a "Rule of Three." If you have a stand-out piece of fabric, position it around the quilt in three places. Three hits of a favorite fabric will create balance and movement.*

3. **Stand back and look.** Stand back at least 10 feet to get a good read on your quilt. Fabrics that don't appear to work up close may look perfect from a few steps back, where you can see their contribution to the design as a whole. Ask yourself: Does it feel balanced? Does my eye move freely around the quilt? Does the mood of the fabrics fit the feeling of the quilt? If you want to, you can prop a fist under your chin like Rodin's *The Thinker* while considering these questions.

[Tip] *Don't get too invested in certain fabrics working out. Many times I've started with an "inspiration fabric," and by the end of the design process, it was the only print not working!*

4. **Don't rush genius.** Continue to experiment with fabric until you feel pleased with your quilt's composition. Really spend some time with your design—this can take anywhere from a few days to a few months. You'll know you've made a masterpiece of scraphazard charm when your design makes you feel nothing short of giddy.

[**Tip**] *Play a wild card. I like to include an unexpected "wild-card" piece of fabric that almost looks like a mistake. Consider placing a wild card in the lower right of your design as a sort of signature. Including the occasional head-scratcher can give your quilts a fresh, unstudied beauty.*

making the quilt

You don't need to be a sewing savant to make a quilt, but it does help to know the basics. From cutting fabric and pressing and piecing together your **quilt top** to basting, quilting, and binding, this section contains everything to guide you through the quilt-making process. Now, ladies and gentlemen . . . to your cutting mats!

CUTTING

The quilts in this book call for 100 percent template-free **rotary cutting**. That means you won't be subjected to the drudgery of tracing around a template with a pencil and cutting out pieces one at a time. The rotary cutting system cuts out multiple pieces quickly and accurately with the help of some simple measuring and a grid.

Rotary cutting ground rules:

Safety on! Make a habit of sliding your rotary cutter's safety guard back into place each time you set it down. Respect the blade!

Always cut away from you. Avoid awkward side-to-side cuts or silly roundabout toward-you cuts.

Good stuff on the left. This is a rule you'll hear quite a bit in rotary cutting, and I interpret it differently than most. When squaring up and when measuring strips, I prefer to place the main body of the fabric on the left, and cut off strips on the right. For me, the "good stuff" is the "most stuff." Find which way feels most intuitive to you.

Measure twice, cut once. This rule from seventh grade woodshop holds true here. Once you've got your ruler in place, check again that your ruler is straight and hitting the measurements you intended.

Cut selvage to selvage. Make cuts on your fabric when it's folded in half lengthwise, with the selvages on top of each other. This is the most efficient, accurate, and tidy way of making cuts.

Before you cut any pieces, you'll need to "square up" your fabric to make sure you're cutting on grain. From there, you'll be on your way to cutting strips, squares, and rectangles.

Squaring up

After you've washed, dried, and ironed your fabric, you are almost ready to start cutting. The first item of business is squaring up your fabric to ensure that you'll be cutting straight-grain strips. To make your quilt fit together accurately, it's important to cut on grain. If you don't, and instead cut on the bias, your fabric may stretch, distort, and create problems for you later in the process.

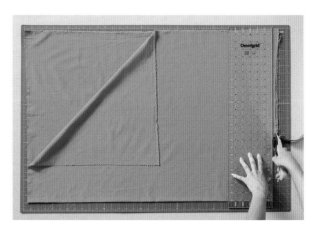

Here's how to kick your cutting off to a great start:

1. Fold the fabric in half, from selvage to selvage. Find your fabric's nice, natural crease, and get the selvages to align as well as possible. This fold should lie flat and not pull to either side. Sometimes a little dance of give-and-take between the selvages and the fold needs to happen. It's often the case that the cut from the fabric store isn't straight and you have to trim off several inches for the fold to lie flat and the selvages to align. If one or both selvages are missing, do your best to determine the fabric's lengthwise grain.

2. Place the fabric on your cutting mat with the fold at the bottom. Carefully align the fold with a horizontal grid line. Place your ruler so that its right edge is near the uneven right edge of the folded fabric. Use the markings on the ruler to make sure the ruler is exactly perpendicular to the fold.

3. Position your left hand firmly on the ruler. Trim off the uneven edge of the fabric with your rotary cutter, placing the blade against the ruler and cutting away from you in one continuous motion. Slowly inch your left hand up along the ruler while maintaining steady pressure. Discard the uneven edge.

NOTE: *Hey you left-handers! Flip steps 2 and 3 on squaring up and adjust the instructions for cutting as needed—they're written for righties.*

Cutting strips

Now that you're assured of cutting your fabric on grain, you're ready to cut strips. If you work on your cutting mat from right to left (like me), rotate the mat so the numbers start in the lower right. Do what feels most natural for you when using the rotary cutting system.

Once you've arranged your mat and squared up your fabric, align the straight, clean edge of the fabric at the 0 on your cutting mat. In this example we'll be cutting a 2½" strip.

Line up your ruler's edge with the 2½" mark on your mat. Using your rotary cutter, cut a 2½" strip. Continue moving your ruler to the left in 2½" increments, aligning it with the grid on your mat and cutting strips.

After you've made a few cuts, you'll need to square up your fabric again so you won't get V-shaped cuts instead of straight ones. The grain line tends to get out of whack with each cut as the fabric shifts slightly.

Cutting squares or rectangles

To cut squares or rectangles, you'll need to first cut a series of strips. Then, take your strips and carefully rotate them on your mat, with the selvages to your right. Stack two or three strips, matching the edges precisely. Align them along the horizontal grid of your cutting mat. Cut off the selvages. Slide your strips over so the right edge is aligned at 0 on your mat. In this example we'll be cutting 2½" x 4½" rectangles.

Line up your ruler's edge with the 4½" mark on your mat. Cut a 4½" rectangle. Continue moving your ruler to the left in 4½" increments, aligning it with the grid on your mat and cutting rectangles.

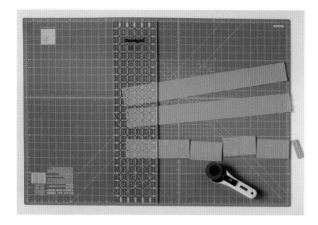

Cutting borders

Borders for your quilt can either be pieced together from shorter lengths of fabric or cut from a single piece of fabric on the lengthwise grain. To make cuts that run parallel—rather than perpendicular—to the selvages, first square up your fabric. Next, fold the fabric into a manageable piece that fits on your cutting mat with the selvages running top to bottom. Finally, cut the border at the proper width using the markings on your mat. Rotate the folded border on your mat, and align it with a horizontal grid. Measure and cut to the proper length.

PIECING

So you've cut out your strips, squares, and rectangles. Now it's time to sew them back together—in different combinations, of course! This process is called piecing your quilt, and it's the step in quilt-making that's the most time-consuming—but it's also satisfying because it's where your quilt top takes shape.

In this section, you'll learn the basics of piecing, which includes chain-piecing and pressing and matching seams. You'll also learn about the "Block Off and Buddy Up" strategy that will help you in the construction of the quilts in this book.

[Tip] *Keep your pieces organized by lining them up in ABC order according to each project's cutting guide. If you think you might confuse the pieces, mark each piece's letter on it with a quilt pencil.*

Stitching guidelines:

Right sides together! Right sides of the fabric pieces should face when sewing.

Long piece on the bottom. If one piece of fabric is slightly longer than the other, sew with the longer piece on the bottom. The feed dogs on your machine will ease in the extra fabric.

Pin at regular intervals. In general, pin your fabric once every 1½" to 2". Start at the ends of the seam, then pin in the middle and continue adding pins between each pin.

Set a moderate stitch length. Nothing so tiny you can't undo, or a stitch so long that it's easy to pull out. A count of 10–12 stitches per inch is best.

Use ¼" seam allowance. Sew a ¼" seam allowance unless told otherwise. This seam allowance is standard in patchwork and quilt-making. Keep the ¼" as accurate and consistent as possible. If you don't have a ¼" quilting foot, measure ¼" away from the needle and mark the throat plate of your machine with a piece of tape to act as a guide.

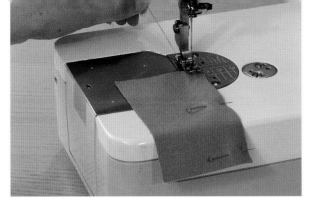

> Hold onto your tail! Hang onto the thread tails when you start sewing to keep them from being sucked into the needle hole and causing a jam.

> Remove pins as you come to them. Never sew over a pin and risk breaking your needle.

> Chain-piece by sewing pairs of pieces one after the other.

No backstitching necessary. Each of the seams will be intersected by another seam, so your threads will be secure.

Tame those threads. Trim threads as you go to keep your patchwork tidy and avoid tangles in your sewing machine.

To start piecing, remove a block from your design wall and arrange it next to your sewing machine according to its pattern diagram. Quilts get pieced one block, or section, at a time. Sometimes I find it helps to take a digital photo of a complicated block before piecing it—the photo provides a reference if pieces get out of order. After the pieces in the block have been arranged in a ready-to-sew position, follow the piecing instructions for each project.

The projects in this book encourage **chain-piecing** pairs of pieces or strips. Chain-piecing (also called quick-piecing or chain-sewing) makes stitching multiple pieces of patchwork together a breeze. This fast and efficient method of piecing has you sewing pairs of pieces continuously without lifting the presser foot or cutting the threads. Just pull a bit of thread through after finishing each seam and start the next piece. When you are finished you'll have a whole chain of pieces, which you snip apart with scissors.

[Tip] *Pre-wind an arsenal of bobbins before you start a new project so you won't lose your sewing momentum.*

Put your mistakes in the past

Use a seam ripper to remove naughty lines of stitching, like crooked pieces or other machine mishaps. Rip through one stitch every ½" on one side of the fabric. Then turn the fabric over and pull out the thread on the opposite side. Make sure to clean up the bits of stray thread left behind before you resume stitching.

Block off and buddy up

Most of the quilts in this book are made up of unique blocks that require piecing on the fly, a method I call the "Block Off and Buddy Up" strategy. Each block gets broken up into units that square off, and within each unit pieces get paired up, sewn together, and then paired up again. Generally, smaller pieces can be joined to become larger rectangular units.

Let's look at a block from the quilt Two Left Feet on page 44. **Block off:** First, arrange the block next to your sewing machine. Divide the block into 3 smaller units that square off.

Round 1: Within these units, buddy up pairs of pieces. Thinking in sensible groupings, create pairs that other pieces will later build upon. Working from left to right and top to bottom, chain-piece the pairs. Remove the chain from your sewing machine. Snip the threads between the units and press.

Round 2: Reposition the sewn pairs in place next to your sewing machine according to the block's diagram. Buddy up the next pairs to be chain-pieced. Working from left to right and top to bottom, chain-piece the pairs. Remove the chain from your sewing machine. Snip the threads between the units and press.

Round 3: Continue to buddy up, chain-piece, and press all available pairs.

Round 4: Continue to buddy up, chain-piece, and press all available pairs.

Round 5: Continue to buddy up, chain-piece, and press all available pairs.

Don't worry—it's hard to screw this up! You'll find the process is rather self-correcting when you try to stitch two pieces together that aren't the same length.

BLOCK OFF

Round 1
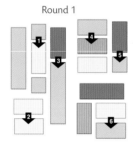

Round 2
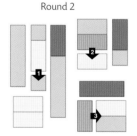

Round 3
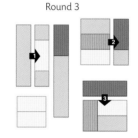

Round 4
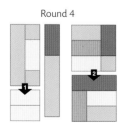

Round 5
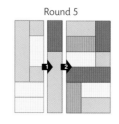

> Pressing seams to one side.

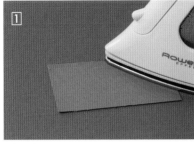 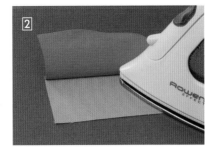 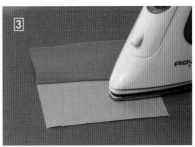

> Pressing seams open.

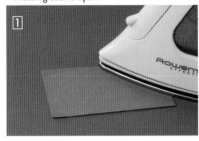  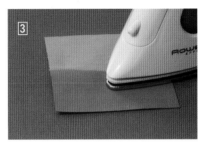

To press seams to one side.

1   Set the seam by pressing seam flat as it was sewn.

2   Position pieces with sewn edge away from your body, with darker piece on top. Lift up top piece and position iron on lighter piece. Move edge of iron against seam.

3   Let edge of darker piece fall backward, and press unit flat.

To press seams to open.

1   Set the seam by pressing seam flat as it was sewn.

2   Work on the fabric's wrong side and use fingers to spread seam open. Insert tip of iron, moving it along seam. Press seam allowances flat.

3   Turn piece right side up and press again.

PRESSING AND MATCHING SEAMS

Pressing is essential to proper piecing. You'll find your ironing board becomes a permanent fixture in your world when piecing a quilt! If you want great results, you should **press** as you sew. Pressing flattens seams and gives you increased accuracy in the size and shape of your patchwork. Because millimeters count, here you'll learn good pressing technique that'll really make a difference in how your quilt comes together.

Pressing is a simple two-step process:

1. **Set the seam.** Press the seam flat as it was sewn, without opening up the fabric pieces. This is a crucial step because it helps the stitches settle into the fabric and makes your seams smooth.

   In piecing, you want to press, not iron. Don't know the difference? Ironing involves dragging the iron back and forth across the fabric, which may stretch or distort your work. A better approach is pressing down on the fabric, picking up the iron, and moving it over before pressing down again. Steam is optional!

2. **Press the seam.** As you press, you're going to have to decide which direction to press your seams. There are two options here: pressing a seam to one side or pressing a

seam open. I can't tell you which way is better, but here you'll read the arguments for both. As you piece, your seams will intersect other seams. If you'd like a professional-looking quilt, you'll want those seam intersections to match up precisely. You're about to see why the way you press your seams is so important to getting precisely matched intersections.

Typically, seams are pressed to one side. Pressing to one side is quick and easy. Because pressing to one side positions a layer of fabric across the seam, it's very durable, and batting is prevented from migrating out between the stitches after the quilt has been assembled. When a seam is pressed so that it matches up with a seam pressed in the opposite direction, it creates an easy-to-align "lock" that quilters love. Ideally, a seam is pressed toward the darker fabric, so it prevents shadows of the darker fabric from showing through the lighter fabric.

Devising a pressing strategy

The way you press your seams is a personal decision. Many of the quilt patterns in this book are positively full of intersecting seams that require matching—and the pressing issue is left entirely up to you. If you want to make the extra effort of pressing your seams open, you'll eliminate the seam matching guesswork entirely. However, if you feel best about pressing your seams to one side, try to think ahead with a pressing plan before you begin piecing. You'll need to balance the two priorities of pressing toward the darker fabric with getting your seams to match up pressed in opposite directions. If it helps, use a pencil to sketch arrows on the project's pattern to indicate the direction you're going to be pressing.

There are many quilters who take the extra time and care to press seams open. They argue that the seam wears more evenly over time, it gives them better precision, and it keeps their quilts smooth and flat. Also, dark shadows are a nonissue when pressing seams open. Many quilters from the "press to one side" camp will press their seams open when dealing with a complex pattern with lots of intersecting seams. Some quilters say, however, that pressing a seam open creates a weaker, more vulnerable seam than pressing to one side. Because machine-piecing creates such durable stitching, the "seams open" camp thinks that point is moot. Whichever way you decide to press your seams will work, as long as you keep pressing!

[Tip] *When pressing your seams to one side, sometimes you can't avoid pressing toward the lighter fabric. In these instances, hand trim about half of the darker fabric's seam allowance to prevent a pesky shadow showing through.*

Matching seams

All that pressing pays off big time when joining pieces to make blocks (or joining blocks to make rows, or joining rows to make a quilt top). Because of your excellent cutting and pressing technique, your intersecting seams should match up. Proper seam alignment will give your quilt slick, expert results.

A straight seam intersection can work one of three ways:

Lock up. Here each seam is pressed to one side—in opposite directions. Seams conveniently nestle into each other, creating an easy-to-align lock. This intersection is nice and flat because pressing in opposite directions distributes the fabric in the seam allowances so there's no extra bulk.

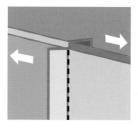

Open up. If you have the patience to painstakingly press your seams open, your intersecting pieces will come together in an easy-to-match package with no fears of bulky seams. Because you've made the extra effort of pressing your seams open, you don't have to sweat how your seams match up.

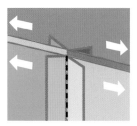

Bulk up. Here two seams pressed in the same direction join forces—and what ensues is added bulk. While you may not win any craftsmanship awards, it won't destroy your quilt, either. A few fat intersections here and there won't ruin your project—they have yet to ruin one of mine. Just use extra care in pinning these intersections to ensure a precise seam match.

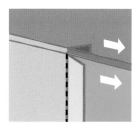

Regardless of the type of seam intersection, insert a pin before and after the seam before sewing. Remove the pins as you sew, being sure the machine's needle touches down on the seam allowance just before each pin, securing the pieces in place.

When sewing, be aware of the seam you can't see on the bottom, taking care that it doesn't get dragged and sewn in the wrong direction. If it starts to fold badly, stop in the needle-down position, lift the presser foot, and flip the seam back in the proper direction. Then lower the presser foot and continue sewing.

ASSEMBLING YOUR QUILT

Once your quilt top is pieced, it's time to advance to the exciting quilt assembly stage. Your quilt isn't yet a quilt until you combine all three layers—quilt top, batting, and backing—into one fluffy masterpiece. From here you are going to baste, quilt, and bind your project, using the instructions that follow. Every quilt and quilted project in this book follows this same set of directions.

Making the "quilt sandwich"
First things first: Gather the quilt top, batting, and backing layers of your quilt.

Quilt top. After you have finished piecing the quilt top, thoroughly press its finished patchwork to achieve a final, flawless finish. Trim stray threads from the back and remove fuzzy debris with a lint roller.

Batting. You want the batting to be bigger than the quilt top. To determine the size you need, measure your quilt top, and then add 5" to the length and width. If you purchased precut batting, remove it from the packaging and unfold it to relax its creases. Read the batting manufacturer's recommendations on minimum quilting intervals before deciding how you'll quilt your project.

Backing. Choose fabrics for your backing that coordinate or complement the colors of your quilt top. A solid-colored backing will emphasize the quilting stitches on your quilt's back, while printed fabrics tend to hide stitches. As with the batting, you'll want a bit of extra fabric extending beyond the quilt top. Measure your quilt top, and then add 5" to the length and width. You can buy massive pieces of cotton fabric especially made for quilt backs in 108" widths, or you can piece your own backing.

For the quilts in this book, I chose a multi-fabric backing, pieced from three horizontal strips. To make this type of quilt back, you need 2 yards each of two fabrics. For the middle strip, trim the selvages off the 2 yards of the first fabric. For the top and bottom strips, trim the selvages off the 2 yards

> To make a quilt sandwich, place backing fabric on a flat work surface, right side down. Smooth out wrinkles from center out, and tape edges of backing to work surface with painter's tape. Center batting on top, again smoothing and taping in place. Finally, position the pressed quilt top in the center, right side up, smoothing it out so it's totally flat.

> To thread-baste a quilt, sew using generous 1" stitches. Baste from the center out in a starburst design, first stitching an "X" from corner to corner and then proceeding with the horizontal and vertical lines from center out. Continue stitching additional lines from the center out until lines are spaced no farther than 3" apart.

of the second fabric, and then cut in half lengthwise. Now sew the 3 pieces together, alternating the fabrics. The backing seams should be parallel to the top and bottom of the quilt top. Press the seams and iron the entire back flat.

With all three layers of the quilt in hand, you need to locate a large, flat surface to spread out all of the layers of your quilt with ease. A clean wood floor or an extra large table work great. Be wary of using carpeting for a work surface—take it from the sucker who pin-basted her quilt right to her carpet . . . twice. If you choose a nice wood floor or table, slide your cutting mat under the bottom of your quilt and move it around as you work, protecting the wood's surface from sharp pins and needles.

BASTING

With the quilt assembled on your work surface, you are ready to baste. Basting temporarily secures the three layers of your quilt together with hand stitches or pins in preparation for the actual quilting. It's crucial that you take your time and baste thoroughly; you don't want the layers of your quilt sandwich to shift or bunch while being subjected to the rolling, folding, and manhandling of the quilting process. As tempting as it may be, don't take shortcuts!

Thread-basting

For quilts, basting with a needle and thread is the best option. You can mark your quilting lines after basting and then sew right over the basting threads. I recommend using a curved quilting needle and a very long strand of thread in a contrasting color so the basting stitches are easy to find and remove after you quilt. Make sure to leave long thread tails at starts and stops. There's no need to tie a knot when threading the needle.

[**Tip**] *To get rid of the holes in your fabric left behind from basting pins or needles, dab a bit of water on the surface and smooth out the fabric with your finger.*

Pin-basting

The other option is pin-basting. However, pin-basting a full-size quilt requires hundreds of pins and leaves you with an unwieldy beast to maneuver and sew quilting lines around. But for smaller projects, basting with bent-arm safety pins is a fast and easy choice. When you're using pins, you have to mark your quilt lines first, so turn to page 32 and map them out before you come back here and insert the pins. Once your quilt lines are drawn, you're ready to insert the pins.

Making sure to stay clear of the quilting lines, pin through all 3 layers, forming a grid of pins 3" to 4" apart. First pin a horizontal and a vertical line through the center. Continue adding pins in the quadrants at the same 3" to 4" interval.

QUILTING

Once the quilt sandwich has been basted, you're ready to stitch all of the layers together. Yes, you are actually at the "quilting" part of the quilt-making process! Quilting adds another element of design to your project and can be as simple or as complex as you'd like.

The most common method of quilting emphasizes the shapes of the patchwork's design with some type of outline stitching. Ever-popular **stitch in the ditch** quilting involves sewing very near the seams in patchwork, highlighting the piecework without really drawing attention to the actual quilt stitches. Similar to this method is **echo quilting,** which follows seam lines at a distance of about ¼", sometimes repeating itself, like ripples, with concentric lines.

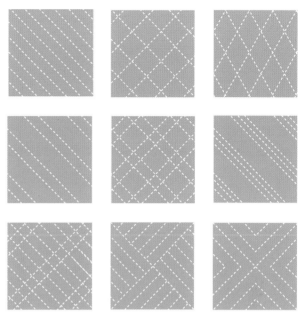

> Just because straight-line geometric designs are easy doesn't mean they're boring! You'd be amazed at the variety of styles you can achieve with simple edge-to-edge stitching.

When to have someone do the quilting for you

Quilting jumbo-size quilts on your home machine is entirely possible—but it's a grueling process. If you find yourself tackling anything larger than a twin-size quilt, I recommend consulting a professional long-arm quilter. **Long-arm quilting machines** are very large (and very expensive) contraptions that accommodate large quilts, securing all of the layers tautly in a frame—eliminating the need for basting. Its "long arm" sewing head moves over the stationary quilt top, stitching simple to very elaborate quilting designs. You can consult your local quilt shop for recommendations on professional long-arm quilters in your area.

> Lay wood molding across the longest diagonal in the center of the quilt, finding the angle of lines you'd like to quilt. Run painter's tape along the edge of the molding, sticking a long strip of tape across the surface of the quilt top from edge to edge.

> Roll the quilt in from two corners, leaving the line to be quilted exposed. Rolling the quilt will tame its bulkiness and help it fit in the throat of your sewing machine.

There are also endless random and highly ordered **all-over quilting** patterns that contrast with the patchwork composition. My favorites are **filler patterns**—simple, geometric quilting designs that are easy to mark and stitch. I absolutely love the dynamic look of diagonal quilting lines, which just so happen to contrast nicely with the straight rectangles and squares in this book's designs.

Marking the quilting lines

Now it's time to mark the lines on your quilt that you'll use to guide your sewing. For small projects, using a ruler and a quilting pencil to mark quilting lines works great. But for large projects like full-size quilts, marking edge-to-edge lines that are straight and equally spaced can be a challenge. I once lined up every ruler I owned end-to-end across a quilt and drew lines alongside them with a quilting pencil.

Needless to say, I only tried that method once! After that I bought a "guide bar" attachment to use with my machine's walking foot that allowed me to mark just one quilting line, stitch over it, and follow each last line of (wobbly) stitching from the guide's set distance. Useful, but still not ideal. Finally, I discovered the ease of using painter's tape to mark quilting lines.

Now my favorite technique for marking straight lines on quilts is using painter's tape along with a piece of wood molding. I run a strip of tape alongside the stable, straight edge of the wood molding to prevent the tape from bowing across a long distance, quilt a perfectly straight line along the edge of the tape, and continue to mark quilt lines and stitch across the surface of the quilt.

When using this method, first decide how far apart you'd like your stitching spaced. If you'd like quilting lines spaced

2" apart, you can buy 2"-wide painter's tape. Many widths of painter's tape are available at your local home-improvement store. You can play with different widths of tape to add variety to your designs.

Stitching quilting lines

After you have marked a quilting line on your quilt, it's finally time to quilt! It helps to spend a little time prepping your sewing area for quilting. Start by screwing on the walking foot attachment to your machine and popping in a fresh bobbin of thread. Clear the table around your sewing machine so your quilt can spread out unhindered.

Starting on the batting at the edge of the quilt top, reduce your machine's stitch length to a very small stitch. Take several tiny stitches from the batting onto the quilt top to secure your thread. Now return to your regular stitch length of 10–12 stitches per inch. Don't pull or stretch the quilt—let the walking foot do its job of advancing the top and bottom layers evenly. When you reach the edge of the quilt, reduce the stitch length again and sew a few stitches to secure your thread. Cut the threads and remove the quilt from the machine.

Stitch the next line along the other edge of the tape. After stitching each side of the tape, move the tape by aligning its edge with the straight line you just sewed, using your wood molding to ensure a straight line. Adjust the quilt "rolls" so that just the area being quilted is exposed. Continue marking and quilting the diagonal lines, completing one half of the quilt at a time. When you are finished quilting, trim off the excess batting and backing, using your rotary cutter and ruler. Remove and discard the basting threads.

[Tip] *Position your ironing board or a table behind you to support the weight of your quilt. This will also help keep the quilt straight and smooth as you guide it through your machine.*

>Throw the quilt over your shoulder and position one end of the taped quilting line under the walking foot. Feed the quilt through the machine little by little, making sure the backing is smooth as you go.

BINDING

Once you've finished quilting, there's only one big step left: covering up the raw edges of the quilt sandwich so they aren't naked and exposed. That is the job of **binding**.

There are several types of binding and several ways to attach it. Traditionally, binding is a two-step ordeal where one side is attached by machine and the other side sewn on by hand. I've never had the patience for this method. I prefer simple **one-step machine-attached binding**: It's not only faster, it uses less fabric, requiring 2" strips of fabric instead of 3". In the book *The Modern Quilt Workshop*, superstar quilters Weeks Ringle and Bill Kerr also advocate this technique because it fits their machine-friendly approach to quilt-making. I couldn't agree more!

Making binding

First, figure out how much binding you'll need. Calculate the perimeter of your quilt by adding the width to the length and multiplying by 2. Add an extra 15" to the total. Now take that number and divide it by 40. (This is the width, in inches, of a strip cut selvage-to-selvage, accounting for shrinkage and trimming the selvages off.) Round up to the next number. This is the number of 2" strips you need to cut. If you are making binding for a quilt in this book, you will need seven 2" strips of fabric cut selvage-to-selvage. Cut the appropriate number of 2" strips and trim off the selvages.

[**Tip**] *I like to make my binding ahead of time—usually when I'm cutting out fabric during the design phase. Making binding can be a welcome break from creative decision-making, and it's great to have it waiting for you after quilting. Wrap your finished binding around a piece of cardboard to keep it flat and organized until you use it.*

Piece the strips together using the following method to make one long continuous strip. This method nicely distributes bulk from seam allowances along the length of your binding:

1. Lay out one strip vertically, right side up. Position the second strip perpendicular to the first strip with its right side down, forming an "L" by matching the corners on the upper right.

    Using a quilting pencil and ruler, draw a line diagonally on the top strip from the top left corner of the lower strip to the bottom right corner of the top strip. Sew along the line. Continue sewing the remaining strips together in the same way.

2. Cut off the corners ¼" from the seams.

3. Press the seams open along the strip (page 27).

4. Using a 1" binding tape maker, feed the end of your strip into the tool, wrong side up. As you pull the fabric

through the tape maker, the raw edges of the fabric strip get folded toward its center. Iron the binding flat as it emerges from the tool.

5. Once the entire strip has gone through the binding tool, fold the strip again in half lengthwise, with the raw edges inside, and press flat.

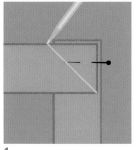

1.

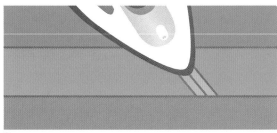

2.

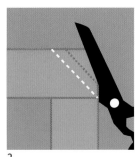

3.

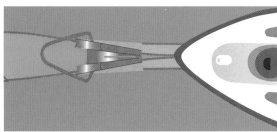

4.

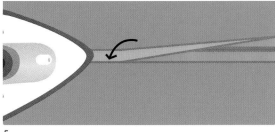

5.

Attaching binding

Once you've made the binding, use the following one-step method to wrap the binding strip over the edges of your quilt and sew it on with one pass through a machine.

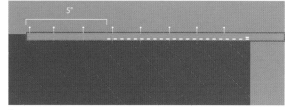

1.

1. Starting on the middle of a long side, snugly wrap the binding around the raw edge of the quilt so it's equal on the front and back sides. Pin in place all the way to one corner. Leaving a 5" loose end (for finishing the binding at the end), sew on top of the binding ⅛" from the inner edge. Make sure you are sewing through both the front and back of the binding simultaneously. Stop sewing ⅛" from the corner, and take a few backstitches. Remove the quilt from the machine and snip the threads.

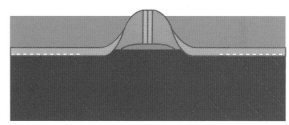

2.

2. To make a corner, bend the strip straight down to the next side of the quilt. Enclose the edge with the two halves of the tape, forming a clean 45-degree miter on the corner. Pin binding in place. Backstitch to secure the thread, and continue sewing to the edge.

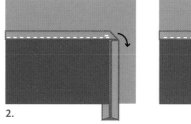

3.

3. Continue sewing the remaining sides, turning the corners as in step 2. After turning the last corner, sew to within 10" of your starting point. Cut the end of the strip, leaving a ½" overlap of the beginning and end of the binding.

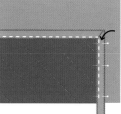

4.

4. Open up both ends of the binding, positioning right sides together. Sew the ends together using a ¼" seam allowance. Use your fingers to press the seam open.

5.

5. Refold the binding lengthwise and position the binding in place, wrapping it around the edge of the quilt. Stitch the remaining section of binding into place, backstitching over a few stitches at the start and stop of the existing sewing.

signing and caring for your quilt

Congratulations! You just made a fun and fabulous quilt! Now all that's left to do is finish it off with your autograph. Always sign your quilts, lest they turn up in a future quilt history book attributed to "Anonymous." On a small piece of fabric, neatly print your name, and possibly the date, city and state, name of your quilt, and who it was made for in permanent marker. You can also design your label on the computer and print it on pretreated fabric sheets available for ink-jet printers. If stitch-work is more your thing, you can hand- or machine-embroider your label. Some sewing shops offer custom machine-embroidered labels for your projects.

To attach the label to your finished quilt, fold the edges of your label under and press. Securely hand-stitch around all four edges of your label, attaching it to the bottom corner of your quilt's back. Use matching thread that won't be visible on the label.

USING YOUR QUILT

Quilts fulfill their special purpose when used throughout the house: on beds for keeping warm, on couches for cuddling during TV marathons, and in children's play areas for use in fort construction. They are usable works of art that should be fully integrated in your day-to-day life. Don't be too concerned about wear and tear on your quilt. If it starts to disintegrate from vigorous overuse, consider your quilt a grand success . . . and make another one!

There is plenty of information on ways to treat your quilt like a delicate textile flower: out of reach of dangerous oily hands, stored in 100 percent cotton pillowcases, away from color-dulling light. If you're the nervous type—or if you made your quilt as a work of art—then quilt preservation methods such as these will be very important to you.

Otherwise, use your quilt! Really, I mean it. When it gets dirty, just machine-wash and dry it. In her terrific book that covers the care of quilts, *From Fiber to Fabric*, Harriet Hargraves recommends using a capful of baby shampoo in cold water on a gentle cycle. To dry, use a low setting. There's

no question that air-drying your quilt will extend its life, but go ahead and machine dry. I won't tell anyone. Few things in life are as lovely as a fresh-smelling and warm quilt out of the dryer. Just enjoy.

> I use embroidered labels for my darker, sillier Quiltsrÿche quilts.

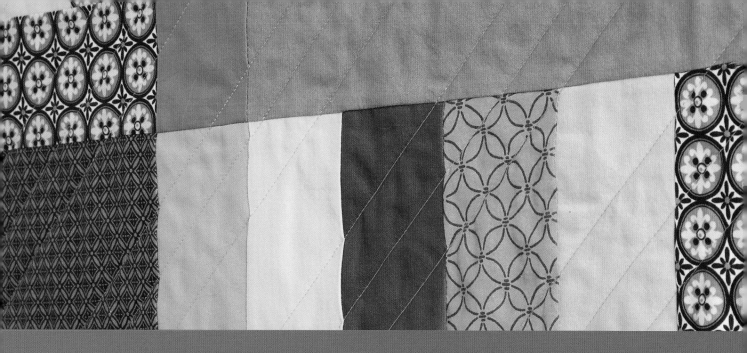

PART 2:
The Quilts

Dare to Be Square quilts are playful updates on traditional patchwork motifs and styles. You're about to see what happens when skulls, deer, and robots meet basket weave, rail fence, and Amish brickwork patterns! These designs meld bold graphic style with stripped-down color schemes, which makes them a cinch to personalize with your own palettes and fabric. You can further break the mold by using project tips on customization and resizing. Because of their square and rectangle compositions, every quilt is a simple-to-stitch, straight-seam dream. Each quilt's pattern and cutting guide will be your most important tools in the construction of your masterpiece. All of the basic techniques required to stitch these projects are covered in Part 1. If you're looking for fast *and* easy, go for the quilts with the lower piece counts. Get ready to make a show-stopping, one-of-a-kind quilt that will stand the test of time. There's something for everyone in these designs!

basket case

Don't waste your short life on soothing colors and fabrics—in this quilt, highly saturated pink and brick create a perfectly frightening color duo. They also help make this quilt equal parts simple, sweet, and sinister! To make the central skull design glow menacingly in low light-light conditions, choose a cool, receding color that creates a bone-chilling contrast with the dynamic and bright basket-weave motif. Basket Case is made for risk-taking, so go for maximum tension and vibrancy.

finished size:	what you need:		
60" x 72"	2 yards solid pink fabric	½ yard assorted prints in	4 yards backing fabric
	2 yards solid brick fabric	pink and brick	Twin-size batting
total pieces:	1 yard solid white fabric	½ yard solid brick binding	
241		fabric	

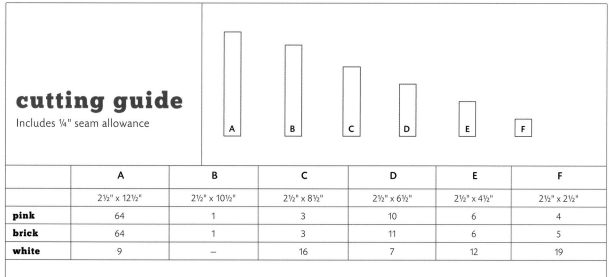

cutting guide
Includes ¼" seam allowance

	A	B	C	D	E	F
	2½" x 12½"	2½" x 10½"	2½" x 8½"	2½" x 6½"	2½" x 4½"	2½" x 2½"
pink	64	1	3	10	6	4
brick	64	1	3	11	6	5
white	9	–	16	7	12	19

For a bigger Basket Case: Repeat BLOCKS 1 and 2 (page 41), alternating their placement to continue the basket-weave pattern. Consult the size chart on page 20.

Cut it out

Using your rotary cutter, ruler, and mat, cut out pieces of your prewashed solid fabric according to the cutting guide.

Mix it up

Position each piece on your design wall according to the pattern diagram. Using the Scraphazard Quilt Design technique described on page 20, replace several solid fabric pieces with print pieces in the corresponding color. Audition a mix of print fabrics by cutting out pieces one by one and swapping them in and out until you've reached a lively balance of plain and patterned. Take your time and enjoy this process!

Piece the blocks

A divide-and-conquer strategy works best for Basket Case. First, focus on the blocks around the perimeter with the straightforward all-A configuration, then focus on the center blocks containing the skull design.

1. Starting with BLOCK 1, arrange the pieces in order next to your sewing machine. Buddy up the pieces into pairs. Working from top to bottom, select the top 2 pieces. Pin and sew. Without cutting the thread or lifting the presser foot, select the next 2 pieces. Pin and sew the pair together right behind the first pair. Continue to sew the last pair to the chain.

    Remove the chain from your sewing machine. Press and cut the threads between the units.

2. Reposition the pairs in order next to your sewing machine. On to Round 2! Sew the first 2 pairs together. Press. Sew on the last pair. Press.

    Square up your block to 12½" x 12½" by pressing and trimming uneven edges with your rotary cutter.

    You've got a completed block! Reposition the block on the design wall and do a victory dance.

When you are ready, repeat the process for BLOCK 2. Continue to work block by block around the quilt's perimeter.

3. Now turn your attention to the more complicated center blocks containing the skull design. Some prep work is in order for these blocks. First you need to sew the smaller pieces into honorary A strips. Starting with BLOCK 7, sew together the E and C pieces to create three 12½" strips. Streamline this process by chain-piecing.

4. Now that you have six 12½" strips (including the 3 A strips), it's business as usual. Just as you did for BLOCK 1, divide the strips into pairs. Align the seams where necessary and carefully pin. Chain-piece the pairs from top to bottom.

    Repeat this process for the remaining center blocks, following the pattern's indication of which pieces get sewn together into the full 12½" strips before assembling each block. Some full strips will be made from 3 or even 4 small pieces.

Sew the blocks into rows

Now that you have 30 blocks, it's time to sew them into 6 rows. Make sure each block is thoroughly pressed. Starting with ROW 1, lay BLOCK 1 on top of BLOCK 2 with right sides together. Secure the 2 blocks with pins. Sew and then press in the direction the seam is leaning naturally. Then sew BLOCK 3 to BLOCK 2, and so on. Press those seams as you go.

Continue sewing the blocks together until you have 6 rows of 5 blocks each.

Based on: Basket weave

A simple basket-weave design is made up of squares sewn from strips, alternately placed horizontally and vertically. This classic configuration produces a checkered pattern similar to that of a woven basket.

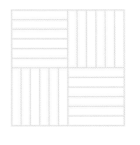

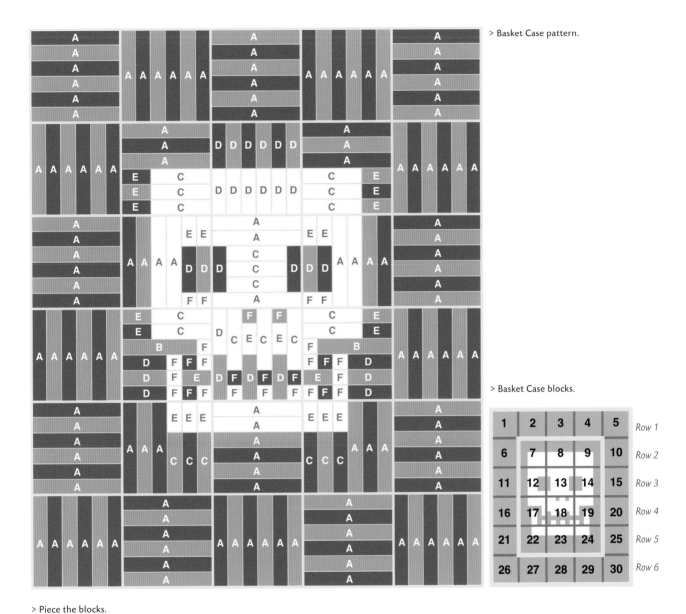

> Basket Case pattern.

> Basket Case blocks.

1	2	3	4	5	*Row 1*
6	7	8	9	10	*Row 2*
11	12	13	14	15	*Row 3*
16	17	18	19	20	*Row 4*
21	22	23	24	25	*Row 5*
26	27	28	29	30	*Row 6*

> Piece the blocks.

Step 1

BLOCK 1
Round 1

Step 2

Round 2

Step 3

BLOCK 7
Round 1

Step 4

Round 2

Round 3

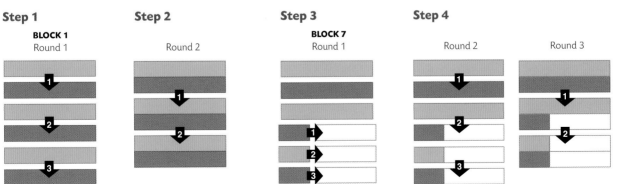

Join the rows together

It's time to sew those rows into one giant quilt top. It's more manageable to first join the rows into 3 groups. Over a long table, spread out ROW 1 and then position ROW 2 on top of it, right sides together. Carefully align the seams, secure the rows with pins, and sew.

Next, sew ROW 3 to 4, and 5 to 6. Now join the 3 massive thirds.

Finish your quilt

Hang your finished quilt top on your design wall. Stand back and admire it. Way to go! Turn to pages 29–35 for instructions on basting, quilting, and binding your quilt.

Vary your cuts on the fly

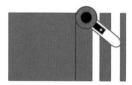 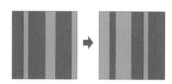

You can easily create a more personalized and irregular Basket Case by varying the width of your cuts on the fly. The pieces in the blocks around the perimeter—and many of the colorful nonskull pieces in the center—can be modified to go from consistent one-size widths to a mixed-up combination of small, medium, and large widths.

While you are cutting your pieces, simply add or subtract 1" to the standard 2½" width using the grid on your cutting mat. Think in blocks or groups. Cut one smaller piece for every piece you cut larger so the units balance out mathematically. For example, to vary the widths of the nonskull pieces in BLOCK 23, cut a 1½" strip, a 3½" strip, and two 2½" strips. When pieced together, they'll be the same width as if you made them all the same 2½" width.

Shuffle the pieces to create variety from block to block.

two left feet

Rock posters have always inspired me. In my many years as a graphic artist, I've watched them evolve from ransom note–style lettering and hand-drawn images to silkscreened masterpieces. In fact, it was a poster by Jesse LeDoux of the design studio Patent Pending Industries that inspired me here; I knew his continuous lines that turned and collided at 90-degree angles were the perfect basis for a quilt! My version features upbeat complementary colors and laid-back neutrals. Here, dark browns create an exaggerated overlap of the bright blue and gold. Mix in monochromatic or low-contrast prints that read as solids from a distance to continue the hypnotic lines without disruption. Prints with pop create a "jump" but can be used sparingly.

finished size:
60" x 72"

total pieces:
304 plus 4 border strips

what you need:

3 yards solid cream fabric
1 yard solid blue fabric
¾ yard solid gold fabric
½ yard solid brown fabric

½ yard assorted prints in
  blue and gold
½ yard solid cream
  binding fabric

4 yards backing fabric
Twin-size batting

cutting guide
Includes ¼" seam allowance

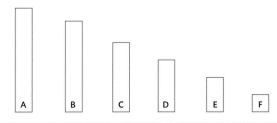

	A	B	C	D	E	F
	2½" x 12½"	2½" x 10½"	2½" x 8½"	2½" x 6½"	2½" x 4½"	2½" x 2½"
cream	14	3	14	21	32	22
blue	1	2	10	13	35	29
gold	2	–	8	10	20	19
brown	1	1	5	4	6	32

Plus: Four 6½" x 60½" cream border strips
For a bigger Two Left Feet: Add one or more sets of 6½"-wide border strips around the perimeter. Consult the size chart on page 20.

Cut it out

Using your rotary cutter, ruler, and mat, cut out pieces of your prewashed solid fabric according to the cutting guide. Cut out the largest pieces first.

Mix it up

Position each piece on your design wall according to the pattern diagram. Using the Scraphazard Quilt Design technique described on page 20, replace several solid fabric pieces with print pieces in the corresponding color. Audition a mix of print fabrics by cutting out pieces one by one and swapping them in and out until you've reached a lively balance of plain and patterned. Take your time and enjoy this process!

Piece the blocks

Get ready to flex your pinning and pressing muscles! This design relies heavily on proper seam alignment to give those lines smooth transitions. Extra time and care with your pins and iron will give you the best results. Piece this quilt one block at a time. Each block is different and requires a unique piecing strategy.

1. Starting with BLOCK 1, arrange the pieces as they appear in the pattern next to your sewing machine. Break the block up into units that square off. You are going to buddy up neighboring pairs of pieces and chain-piece these pairs in a logical order. For more on this Block Off and Buddy Up approach, turn to page 26.

2. Starting on the block's left side, select a pair of pieces. Pin and sew. Don't cut the thread or lift the presser foot just yet! Working left to right, select another pair of pieces. Pin and sew. Continue to move across the block, chain-piecing all available pairs.

   Remove the chain from your sewing machine. Press and cut the threads between the units.

3. Reposition the sewn pairs next to your sewing machine according to the pattern diagram's BLOCK 1 configuration. On to the next round! Now buddy up each joined piece to a neighboring piece within the same unit. Pin, chain-piece, and press.

4. Continue this process using the Block Off and Buddy Up strategy. Perform several rounds of buddying up, chain-piecing, and pressing until the block is completed.

   Square up your block to 12½" x 12½" by pressing and trimming uneven edges with your rotary cutter. You've got a completed block! Reposition the block on the design wall.

When you are ready, repeat the piecing steps for BLOCK 2. Don't worry—it's hard to screw this up! You'll find the process is rather self-correcting when you try to stitch two pieces together that aren't the same length. Continue to work block by block through all 20 blocks.

> Piece the blocks.

Step 1

BLOCK 1

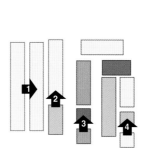

Step 2   **Step 3**   **Step 4**

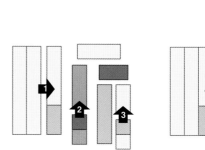

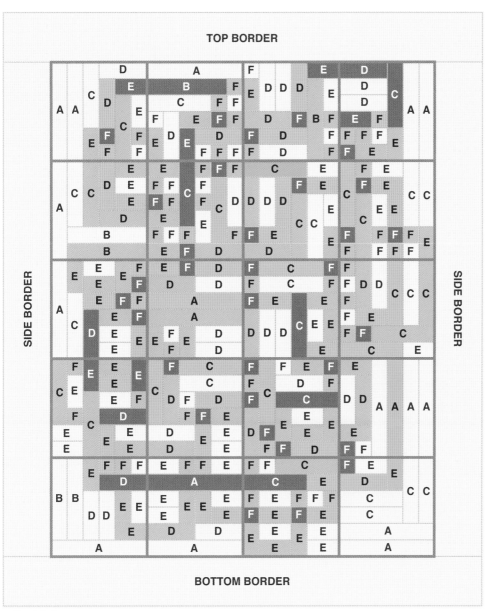

> Two Left Feet pattern.

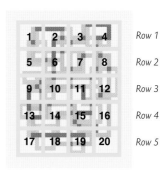

> Two Left Feet blocks.

Sew the blocks into rows

Now that you have 20 blocks, it's time to sew them into 5 rows. Make sure each block is thoroughly pressed. Starting with ROW 1, lay BLOCK 1 on top of BLOCK 2 with right sides together. Take your time and carefully match the seam intersections. Secure the 2 blocks with pins. Sew and press. Then sew BLOCK 3 to BLOCK 2, and so on. Continue sewing the blocks together until you have 5 rows of 4 blocks each.

Join the rows together

It's time to sew those rows into one giant quilt top. It's more manageable to first join the rows into 2 groups. Over a long table, spread out ROW 1 and position ROW 2 on top of it, right sides together. Carefully align the seams and secure the rows with pins. Now take a deep breath and sew.

Next, sew ROWS 3 to 4, and 5 to 4. Now join the 2 groups. Be sure to press those seams as you go.

Add borders

With right sides together, pin two 6½" x 60½" border strips to the sides of the quilt top.

Sew and press the seams toward the border.

Repeat to add top and bottom borders.

Finish your quilt

Hang your finished quilt top on your design wall. Stand back and admire it. Way to go! Turn to pages 29–35 for instructions on basting, quilting, and binding your quilt.

Based on: Gordian knot

Got a complicated or unsolvable problem? You've got a gordian knot. This conundrum is often represented by a knotty puzzle with no visible beginning or end. Many quilted variations of this motif use squares, rectangles, and clever color placement to create the illusion of an unending line, often tilted at a 45-degree angle (or in quilting lingo, "on point").

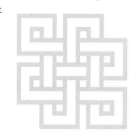

does not compute

Warning! Warning! Worlds collide when robot technology meets a traditional Amish brickwork design. The colors also collide: I wanted the vibrant blues of this retro robot to pop against the stairstep background, so I chose currents of complementary orange for maximum contrast. The background design does command a lot of attention, so stick with light to medium values that won't overpower your gentle robot. I selected a simple two-color stairstep pattern, but you can add additional steps of light- to mid-value color. Modulate the futuristic tone by adding bits of plaid or other prints in different scales.

finished size:	what you need:		
60" x 72"	2 yards solid light orange fabric	½ yard dark blue fabric	½ yard solid medium orange binding fabric
total pieces:	2 yards solid medium orange fabric	⅛ yard bright red-orange fabric	4 yards backing fabric
523	¾ yard medium blue fabric	½ yard assorted prints in light and medium orange	Twin-size batting

cutting guide
Includes ¼" seam allowance

	A	B	C	D	E	F	G	H
	2½" x 4½"	2½" x 2½"	2½" x 6½"	2½" x 8½"	2½" x 12½"	1½" x 4½"	1½" x 2½"	2" x 2½"
light orange	204	12	4	–	–	–	–	2
medium orange	206	14	2	–	–	–	–	–
medium blue	13	4	6	2	9	–	–	–
dark blue	16	5	6	1	5	–	1	–
red-orange	3	3	1	–	–	2	2	–

To simplify this quilt, refer to Boost Your Efficiency with Strip-Piecing, page 54.
For a bigger Does Not Compute: Repeat BLOCKS 1 and 2 (page 53), alternating their placement to continue the stairstep pattern. Adjust the colors as necessary. Consult the size chart on page 20.

Cut it out

Using your rotary cutter, ruler, and mat, cut out pieces of your prewashed solid fabric according to the cutting guide. Cut out the largest pieces first.

Mix it up

Position each piece on your design wall according to the pattern diagram. Using the Scraphazard Quilt Design technique described on page 20, replace several solid fabric pieces with print pieces in the corresponding color. Audition a mix of print fabrics by cutting out pieces one by one and swapping them in and out until you've reached a lively balance of plain and patterned. Take your time and enjoy this process!

Piece the blocks

A divide-and-conquer strategy works best for Does Not Compute. First, focus on the blocks around the perimeter with the straightforward all-A configuration, then move to the center blocks with the robot design.

Starting with BLOCK 1, arrange the pieces as they appear in the pattern next to your sewing machine. Divide the block into 3 rows, buddying up neighboring pairs of pieces. (If you've used the strip-piecing technique, the buddying up has already been done for you! Skip to step 2.)

1. Starting in the block's upper left, select a pair of pieces. Pin and sew. Working left to right, select another pair of pieces. Pin and sew. Continue to move left to right and up to down across the block, chain-piecing all pairs.

    Remove the chain from your sewing machine. Press and snip the threads between the units.

2. Reposition the sewn pairs next to your sewing machine according to the pattern diagram's BLOCK 1 configuration. From the upper left, buddy up the joined pair to the neighboring pair on its right. Pin and sew. Now skip to the row below it, selecting the leftmost pair and sewing it to the pair to its right. Skip again to the row below it for the left two pairs.

Remove the chain from your sewing machine. Press and snip the threads between the units.

3. Again, reposition the sewn pairs next to your sewing machine. Finish sewing the joined pairs into 3 rows.

4. Sew the 3 rows together.

    Square up your block to 12½" x 12½" by pressing and trimming uneven edges with your rotary cutter. Reposition the block on the design wall.

Repeat the piecing steps for BLOCK 2—note that it's configured a little differently from BLOCK 1. Continue to work through the blocks around the perimeter with the straightforward all-A configuration. BLOCKS 10, 16, 21, 27, and 29 have 2 B pieces that are sewn together to form an A-size piece, but otherwise the process is the same as for BLOCK 1.

Now turn your attention to the center blocks containing the robot design. BLOCKS 7, 9, 18, and 24 can be broken into 3 rows and pieced exactly like the perimeter blocks.

Each remaining block is different and requires a unique piecing strategy. Starting with BLOCK 8, arrange the pieces as they appear in the pattern next to your sewing machine. Perform several rounds of buddying up, chain-piecing, and pressing until the block is completed.

Piece the remaining robot blocks using this Block Off and Buddy Up strategy (page 26).

Based on: Amish brickwork

This clever pairing of rectangles creates a bold stairstep pattern that travels diagonally across the quilt. This pattern creates a dynamic zigzag design called Streak of Lightning when tilted at a 45-degree angle.

> Piece the blocks.

Step 1

BLOCK 1

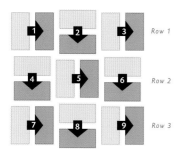

Row 1

Row 2

Row 3

Step 2

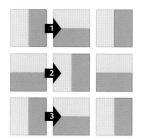

Step 3

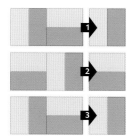

Step 4

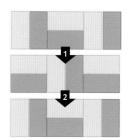

> Does Not Compute pattern.

> Does Not Compute blocks.

1	2	3	4	5	Row 1
6	7	8	9	10	Row 2
11	12	13	14	15	Row 3
16	17	18	19	20	Row 4
21	22	23	24	25	Row 5
26	27	28	29	30	Row 6

Sew the blocks into rows

Now that you have 30 blocks, it's time to sew them into 6 rows. Make sure each block is thoroughly pressed. Starting with ROW 1, lay BLOCK 1 on top of BLOCK 2 with right sides together. Secure the 2 blocks with pins. Sew and press. Then sew BLOCK 3 to BLOCK 2, and so on. Be sure to press seams as you go.

Continue sewing the blocks together until you have 6 rows of 5 blocks each.

Join the rows together

Spread out ROW 1 and then position ROW 2 on top of it, right sides together. Carefully align the seams, secure the rows with pins, and sew. Next, sew ROWS 3 to 4, and 5 to 6. Now sew together the 3 groups.

Finish your quilt

Hang your finished quilt top on your design wall. Turn to pages 29–35 for instructions on basting, quilting, and binding your quilt.

Boost your efficiency with strip-piecing

	A	SUPER STRIP	
	2½" x 4½"	2½" x 18"	
light orange	6	50	
medium orange	8	50	

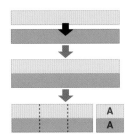

If you'd like to try an alternative time-saving method, try strip-piecing! This method does the buddying up for you. Simply reduce the cutting recipe for the light and medium orange A pieces, and add 50 "super strips" of each.

Chain-piece the strips together until you have 50 joined super strips. Cut each super strip unit into four 4½" lengths. Retain the light and medium orange A pieces for use in the blocks that include part of the robot.

quilt in the headlights

Deer me! Is that a handsome 18-point buck on your bed? Sleeping stag just got fun with this new modern-rustic classic. Let your deer run wild in a field of low-contrast pale blues or other light-colored fabrics. Pay attention to the stairstep "paths" that form when the same fabrics touch at right angles, and distribute them around the quilt to create movement. Replace some of the blue pieces with bold accent fabrics like red and bright yellow for some excitement in an otherwise serene setting. These attention-grabbers look best when working *with* the antlers, so make them touch the antler pieces by running them parallel or attaching them perpendicularly.

finished size:	what you need:		
60" x 72½"	4 yards light blue fabric in 4 shades	½ yard solid medium brown fabric	½ yard solid red binding fabric
total pieces:	¾ yard solid dark brown fabric	½ yard solid black fabric	4 yards backing fabric
212		1½ yards assorted prints in browns, blues, and additional accents	Twin-size batting

cutting guide

Includes ¼" seam allowance

	A	B	C	D	E	F
	3" x 15½"	3" x 13"	3" x 10½"	3" x 8"	3" x 5½"	3" x 3"
dark brown	2	2	6	10	13	4
medium brown	2	3	2	–	5	1
black	–	2	3	4	5	4
medium blue-gray	1	3	2	10	3	1
medium blue	4	1	11	10	10	1
light blue-gray	5	4	8	16	4	2
light blue	4	6	14	11	10	3

For a bigger Quilt in the Headlights: Repeat BLOCK 17 (page 59) along the sides and top. Alternate vertically and horizontally to create an imperfect rail fence stairstep effect. Consult the size chart on page 20.

Cut it out

Using your rotary cutter, ruler, and mat, cut out pieces of your prewashed solid fabric according to the cutting guide.

Mix it up

Position each piece on your design wall according to the pattern diagram. Using the Scraphazard Quilt Design technique described on page 20, replace several solid fabric pieces with print pieces in the corresponding color or trade out for a bright accent. Audition a mix of print fabrics by cutting out pieces one by one and swapping them in and out until you've reached a lively balance of plain and patterned. Take your time and enjoy this process!

Piece the blocks

Get ready to flex your pinning and pressing muscles! This design relies on proper seam alignment to give those antlers smooth transitions. Extra time and care with your pins and iron will give you the best results.

1. Tackle the piecing block by block. Each block is different and requires a unique piecing strategy. Starting with BLOCK 1, arrange the pieces as they appear in the pattern next to your sewing machine. Break the block up into units that square off. You are going to buddy up neighboring pairs of pieces and chain-piece these pairs in a logical order. For more on the Block Off and Buddy Up approach, turn to page 26.

2. Starting on the block's left side, select a pair of pieces. Carefully pin and sew. Don't cut the thread or lift the presser foot just yet! Working left to right, select another pair of pieces. Pin and sew. Continue to move across the block, chain-piecing all available pairs.

    Remove the chain from your sewing machine. Press and cut the threads between the units.

3. Reposition the sewn pairs next to your sewing machine according to the pattern diagram's BLOCK 1 configuration. On to the next round! Now buddy up the next set of pairs. Pin, chain-piece, and press.

4. One last time, reposition the sewn pairs next to your sewing machine. Pin and sew the remaining units into one block.

    Square up your block by pressing and trimming uneven edges with your rotary cutter. You've got a completed block!

    Position the block on the design wall.

Based on: Rail fence

A simple rail fence is made of three fabric strips in a square. The squares are alternated vertically and horizontally to create a stairstep pattern.

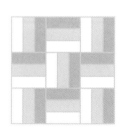

> Piece the blocks.

Step 1

BLOCK 1

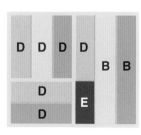

Step 2

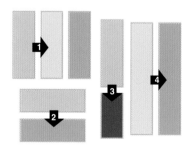

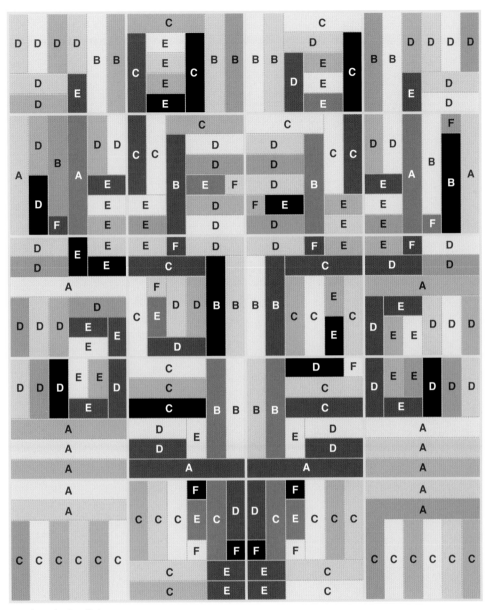

> Quilt in the Headlights pattern.

> Quilt in the Headlights blocks.

Step 3

Step 4

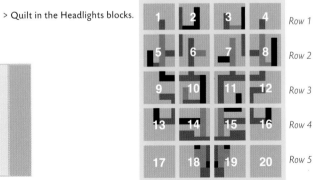

1	2	3	4	*Row 1*
5	6	7	8	*Row 2*
9	10	11	12	*Row 3*
13	14	15	16	*Row 4*
17	18	19	20	*Row 5*

When you are ready, repeat this process with BLOCK 2. Don't worry—it's hard to screw this up! You'll find the process is rather self-correcting when you try to stitch 2 pieces together that aren't the same length.

Continue to work block by block through all 20 blocks using the Block Off and Buddy Up strategy (page 26) by performing several rounds of buddying up, chain-piecing, and pressing until each block is completed.

Sew the blocks into rows

Now that you have 20 blocks, it's time to sew them into 5 rows. Make sure each block is thoroughly pressed. Starting with ROW 1, lay BLOCK 1 on top of BLOCK 2 with right sides together. Secure the two blocks with pins. Sew and press. Then sew BLOCK 3 to BLOCK 2, and so on.

Continue sewing the blocks together until you have 5 rows of 4 blocks each. Pay attention to where the antler seams intersect, and pin carefully to ensure smooth transitions as you sew!

Join the rows together

It's more manageable to first join the rows into 3 groups. Over a long table, spread out ROW 1 and then position ROW 2 on top of it, right sides together. Carefully align the seams, paying special attention to where the antler seams intersect. Secure the rows with pins. Now take a deep breath and sew.

Next, sew ROW 3 to 4. Now join the 2 groups to each other and ROW 5. Be sure to press seams as you go.

Finish your quilt

Hang your finished quilt top on your design wall. Stand back and admire it. Way to go! Turn to pages 29–35 for instructions on basting, quilting, and binding your quilt.

Break free from the pattern

You don't need to follow this (or any) pattern exactly as written! With a pattern that uses lots of long pieces, such as Quilt in the Headlights, you can easily customize your quilt by breaking the longer pieces into several shorter ones. Adding additional pieces in different fabrics will increase your quilt's lovable scrappiness and make it uniquely yours. Just make sure your quilt's design motif still reads clearly!

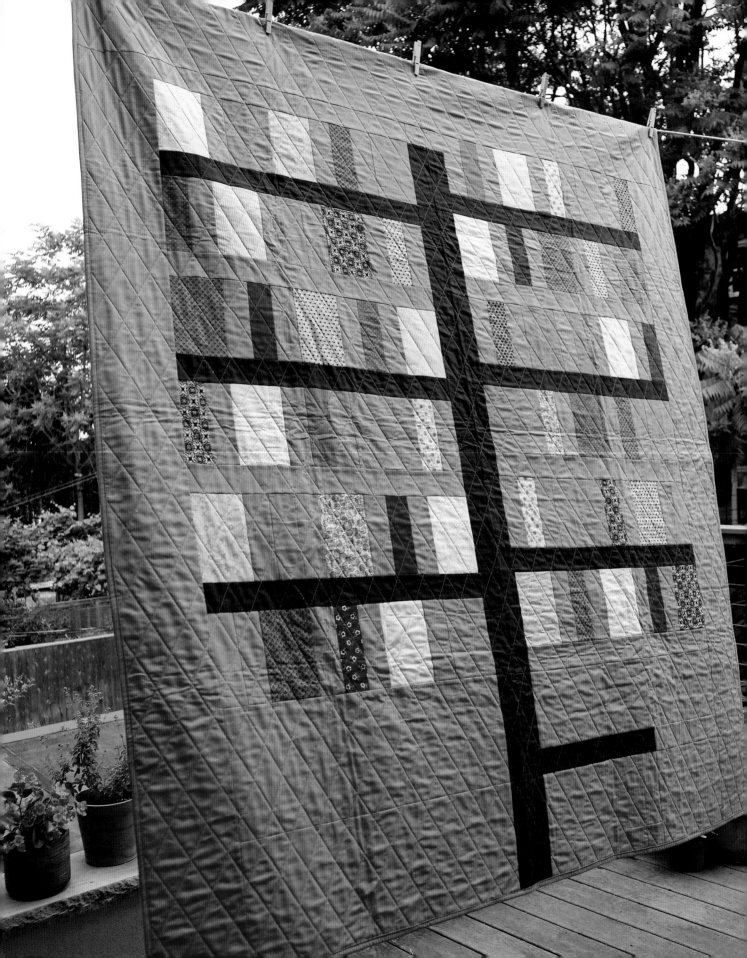

love it or leaf it

Bring the outside indoors with this deciduous delight! Love It or Leaf It turns a stacked-coins design on its side, transforming your long-suffering scraps into lively leaves. I wanted a color palette that produced a dreamlike tree that's more surreal than seasonal. As you can see, pink provides an unexpected backdrop for a medley of autumnal-hued scraps in cream, orange, and rust. However, a literal approach would look equally cheeky in vibrant spring greens under a blue sky. Either way, this super-simple project will have you curled up under polka-dotted and plaid foliage in no time.

finished size:	what you need:	½ yard assorted prints in
64" x 72"	3 yards solid pink fabric	orange and cream
	¾ yard solid charcoal fabric	½ yard solid pink binding
total pieces:	¾ yard solid cream fabric	fabric
155 plus 3	½ yard solid orange fabric	4 yards backing fabric
border strips		Twin-size batting

cutting guide

Includes ¼" seam allowance

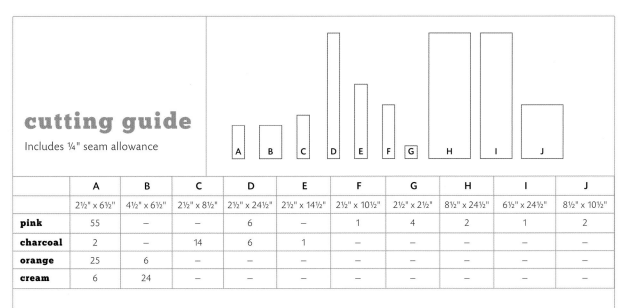

	A	B	C	D	E	F	G	H	I	J
	2½" x 6½"	4½" x 6½"	2½" x 8½"	2½" x 24½"	2½" x 14½"	2½" x 10½"	2½" x 2½"	8½" x 24½"	6½" x 24½"	8½" x 10½"
pink	55	–	–	6	–	1	4	2	1	2
charcoal	2	–	14	6	1	–	–	–	–	–
orange	25	6	–	–	–	–	–	–	–	–
cream	6	24	–	–	–	–	–	–	–	–

Plus: One 8½" x 64½" pink top border strip and two 6½"x 64½" pink side border strips.
For a bigger Love It or Leaf It: Add one or more sets of 6½"-wide border strips around the perimeter. Consult the size chart on page 20.

Cut it out

Using your rotary cutter, ruler, and mat, cut out pieces of your prewashed solid fabric according to the cutting guide. Cut out the largest pieces first.

Mix it up

Position each piece on your design wall according to the pattern diagram. Using the Scraphazard Quilt Design technique described on page 20, replace several solid fabric pieces with print pieces in the corresponding color. Audition a mix of print fabrics by cutting out pieces one by one and swapping them in and out until you've reached a lively balance of plain and patterned. Take your time and enjoy this process!

Piece the blocks

Love It or Leaf It is an extremely forgiving pattern with minimal seam intersections. All of the "leaf blocks" (BLOCKS 1–12) are pieced in the same way, with the remaining blocks (13–16) requiring very little stitching.

> Piece the blocks.

1. Starting with BLOCK 1, arrange the pieces in order next to your sewing machine. Buddy up the A and B pieces—the "leaves"—into pairs.

2. Select the first pair and position the right sides together. Carefully pin and sew, select the next 2 pieces, and pin and sew the pair together right behind the first pair. Continue to chain-piece the remaining pairs to the chain.

   Remove the chain from your sewing machine. Press and snip the threads between the units.

3. Reposition the pairs in order next to your sewing machine. Buddy up the joined pairs into new units of two. Chain-piece the new pairs together. Press.

4. One last time, reposition the joined units in order next to your sewing machine. Sew the 3 joined units together. Press.

5. Sew together the D and G pieces into one strip. Press. Now sew the long strip along the top of the single unit of leaf pieces.

Step 1

BLOCK 1

Step 2

Step 3

Step 4

Step 5

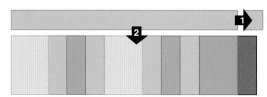

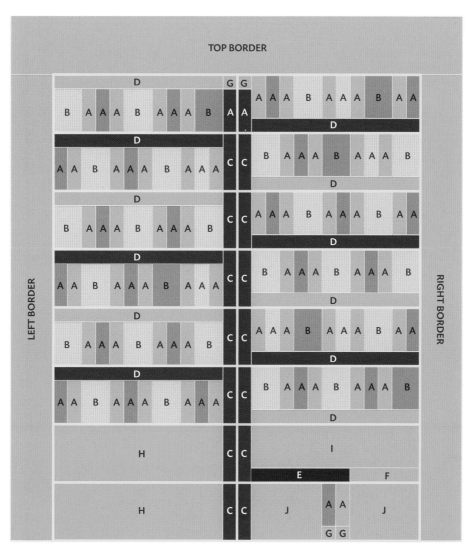

> Love It or Leaf It pattern.

> Love It or Leaf It blocks.

Left half   Right half

[Tip] *Have some charming scraps that aren't quite big enough to be A pieces? Stitch together a "Franken-piece" from several scraps, then use a rotary cutter to trim to a perfect and totally unique A piece.*

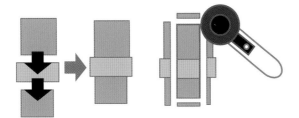

Square up your block to 26½" x 8½" by pressing and trimming uneven edges with your rotary cutter. Position the block on the design wall.

Repeat the process, working block by block through all 16 blocks. Note that for BLOCKS 3–12 you'll need to sew the D piece to the "leaves" before sewing the C piece to the end of the block. For BLOCKS 14 and 16, sew the pieces into sensible units, referring to the Block Off and Buddy Up strategy on page 26.

Sew the blocks into halves

Make sure each block is thoroughly pressed. Starting with the left half, lay BLOCK 1 on top of BLOCK 3 with right sides together. Carefully match the seam intersection at the "trunk." Secure the two blocks with pins. Sew and then press. Repeat this for BLOCKS 5 and 7, 9 and 11, and 13 and 15.

Now that you have 4 pieced pairs of blocks, join them together in order.

Repeat this process for the right side, sewing BLOCK 2 to 4, 6 to 8, 10 to 12, and 14 to 16. Then join the block pairs.

Join the two halves

It's time to join those halves into one giant quilt top. Over a long table, spread out the left half and then position the right half on top of it, right sides together. Carefully align the seams and secure the halves with pins. Now take a deep breath and sew. Yes! You've joined all of the blocks.

Add borders

With right sides together, pin one of the 6½" x 64½" border strips to each side of the quilt top. Sew and press the seams toward the border.

Repeat to add the 8½" x 64½" border along the top of the quilt.

Finish your quilt

Hang your finished quilt top on your design wall. Stand back and admire it. Way to go! Turn to pages 29-35 for instructions on basting, quilting, and binding your quilt.

Based on: Stacked Coins

In this scrappy classic, the "coins" are assembled from random colors and lengths of horizontal strips and set off by alternating plain sashes. Also called Chinese coins, this design is a less stuffy version of a stark and simple Amish bar quilt.

chatterbox

In this exuberant design, a quiet four-patch block has quite a bit to say: When its four squares are scaled to different proportions in a staggered brickwork composition, they shout back in a lively back-and-forth conversation. When I imagine yellow and gray engaged in conversation, yellow is the lighthearted optimist giving glass-half-empty gray a pep talk. What color duo suits the personalities of you and the person you love chatting with most? Any color coupling will work, just frame the talk bubbles in white, black, or another cool, receding color. If you'd like a noisier Chatterbox, add additional pairs of colors and alternate the columns.

finished size:	what you need:		
60" x 72"	2 yards solid white fabric	1 yard assorted prints in	4 yards backing fabric
	1⅝ yards solid	yellow and gray	Twin-size batting
total pieces:	yellow fabric	½ yard solid white	
198	1⅝ yards solid gray	binding fabric	
	fabric		

cutting guide
Includes ¼" seam allowance

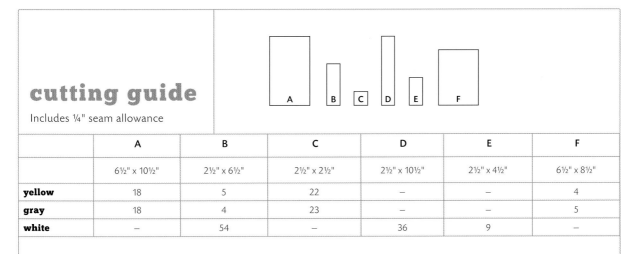

	A	B	C	D	E	F
	6½" x 10½"	2½" x 6½"	2½" x 2½"	2½" x 10½"	2½" x 4½"	6½" x 8½"
yellow	18	5	22	–	–	4
gray	18	4	23	–	–	5
white	–	54	–	36	9	–

For a bigger Chatterbox: Add alternating replicas of ROWS 1 and 2 to expand the quilt vertically, and insert additional replicas of BLOCK 2 (page 71) in each row's center to expand the quilt horizontally. Adjust the colors as necessary. Consult the size chart on page 20.

Cut it out

Using your rotary cutter, ruler, and mat, cut out pieces of your prewashed solid fabric according to the cutting guide.

Mix it up

Position each piece on your design wall according to the pattern diagram. Using the Scraphazard Quilt Design technique described on page 20, replace several solid fabric pieces with print pieces in the corresponding color. Audition a mix of print fabrics by cutting out pieces one by one and swapping them in and out until you've reached a lively balance of plain and patterned. Take your time and enjoy this process!

Piece the blocks

Work the piecing for Chatterbox row-by-row, chain-piecing two blocks at a time. Because there are no seams to match, these blocks sew up quickly.

Starting with BLOCKS 1 and 2, arrange the pieces in order next to your sewing machine.

1. Select the B pieces from BLOCK 1 and position the right sides together. Carefully pin and sew. Without cutting the thread or lifting the presser foot, select the A and B pieces of BLOCK 2. Pin and sew. Continue to chain-piece piece C to piece D.

   Remove the chain from your sewing machine. Press and snip the threads between the units.

2. Reposition the pairs in order next to your sewing machine. Sew the B unit from BLOCK 1 to the E piece. Without breaking the chain, sew the A and B unit from BLOCK 2 to the C and D unit. Press each block.

3. Next, sew BLOCK 1 to BLOCK 2.

   Square up your joined blocks by pressing and trimming uneven edges with your rotary cutter. You've got 2 completed blocks! Reposition them on the design wall.

When you are ready, piece BLOCKS 3 and 4 in a similar way, and then 5 and 6. Continue to work through the blocks in units of 2, going row by row.

Sew the blocks into rows

Now that you have 27 units of 54 blocks, it's time to sew them into 9 rows. Make sure each block is thoroughly pressed. Starting with ROW 1, join the 3 units into one row. With right sides together, lay BLOCKS 1 and 2 on top of BLOCKS 3 and 4. Secure the 2 units with pins. Sew and then press. Next, sew on BLOCKS 5 and 6.

Continue sewing the blocks together until you have 9 rows of 3 units (6 blocks) each.

Join the rows together

It's time to sew those rows into one giant quilt top. It's more manageable to first join the rows into 3 groups. Over a long table, spread out ROW 1 and then position ROW 2 on top of it, right sides together. Secure the rows with pins. Now take a deep breath and sew. Next, sew on ROW 3.

Next, join ROWS 4, 5, and 6, then ROWS 7, 8, and 9. Now join the 3 groups. Be sure to press seams as you go.

Finish your quilt

Hang your finished quilt top on your design wall. Stand back and admire it. Way to go! Turn to pages 29–35 for instructions on basting, quilting, and binding your quilt.

Based on: Four patch

The classic four-patch block is probably the simplest of all patchwork configurations, providing the basis for many well-known patterns. It consists of four squares joined in pairs and relies on contrast between light and dark to create interest.

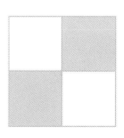

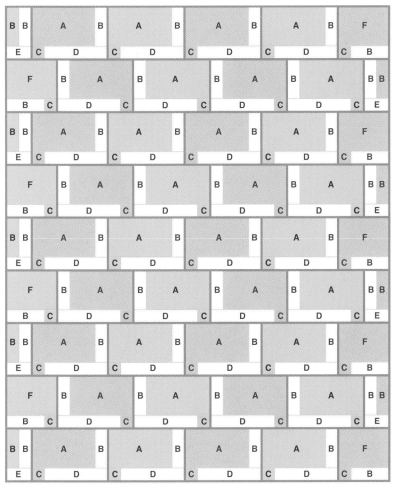

> Chatterbox pattern.

Give 'em something to talk about

Want a more personalized Chatterbox? Add bits of conversation inside the talk bubbles! Do you and your sweetheart have signature sleepy sign-offs when late-night IMing? Is there a ridiculous exchange between you and your BFF that will go down in infamy? Or would you find it therapeutic to commemorate the rise and fall of a romance by stitching your entire text message history? Make this quilt a cozy chronicle of your chatty transactions!

First, decide on the dialogue. Make sure each short blurb will fit comfortably within a 10½" x 6½" A piece. Then, use embroidery, fabric paint and stencils, fabric markers, or ink-jet transfers to embellish your quilt. For recommended reading on these techniques, visit the Resources section on page 157.

> Chatterbox blocks.

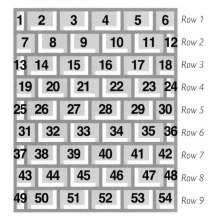

1	2	3	4	5	6	Row 1
7	8	9	10	11	12	Row 2
13	14	15	16	17	18	Row 3
19	20	21	22	23	24	Row 4
25	26	27	28	29	30	Row 5
31	32	33	34	35	36	Row 6
37	38	39	40	41	42	Row 7
43	44	45	46	47	48	Row 8
49	50	51	52	53	54	Row 9

> Piece the blocks.

Step 1

BLOCK 1 **BLOCK 2**

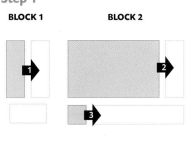

Step 2

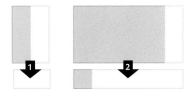

Step 3

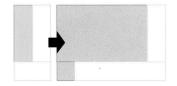

snooze button

Wake up, sleepyhead! Okay, you can sleep just a little bit longer . . . this quilt's so cozy after all. But just because Snooze Button is the perfect companion for the championship sleeper in your life, that doesn't mean you should press snooze on these bright colors! Wake up the fabrics in your alarm clock by choosing a cool, receding color like navy blue to frame them. Work in graphic, youthful prints like polka dots and stripes around the clock's face, alternating light and dark values. For extra buzz, go with an unpredictable, scraphazard arrangement of fabrics.

finished size:
62" x 72"

total pieces:
136
plus 3 border strips

what you need:
3 yards solid navy blue fabric
¾ yard solid bright blue fabric
¾ yard solid cream fabric
⅓ yard solid lime green fabric
¼ yard solid orange fabric

¼ yard solid red fabric
⅛ yard solid black fabric for clock hands
1 yard assorted prints in navy, bright blue, cream, lime green, orange, and red

½ yard solid lime green binding fabric
4 yards backing fabric
Twin-size batting

cutting guide
Includes ¼" seam allowance

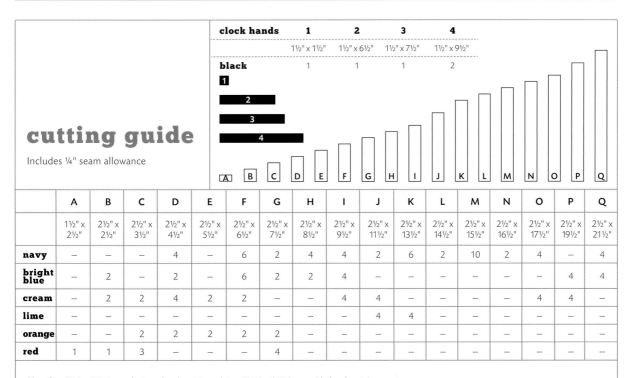

clock hands	1	2	3	4
	1½" x 1½"	1½" x 6½"	1½" x 7½"	1½" x 9½"
black	1	1	1	2

	A	B	C	D	E	F	G	H	I	J	K	L	M	N	O	P	Q
	1½" x 2½"	2½" x 2½"	2½" x 3½"	2½" x 4½"	2½" x 5½"	2½" x 6½"	2½" x 7½"	2½" x 8½"	2½" x 9½"	2½" x 11½"	2½" x 13½"	2½" x 14½"	2½" x 15½"	2½" x 16½"	2½" x 17½"	2½" x 19½"	2½" x 21½"
navy	–	–	–	4	–	6	2	4	4	2	6	2	10	2	4	–	4
bright blue	–	2	–	2	–	6	2	2	4	–	–	–	–	–	–	4	4
cream	–	2	2	4	2	2	–	–	4	4	–	–	–	–	4	4	–
lime	–	–	–	–	–	–	–	–	–	4	4	–	–	–	–	–	–
orange	–	–	2	2	2	2	2	–	–	–	–	–	–	–	–	–	–
red	1	1	3	–	–	–	4	–	–	–	–	–	–	–	–	–	–

Plus: One 8½" x 62½" navy bottom border strip and two 10½" x 64½" navy side border strips.
For a bigger Snooze Button: Add one or more sets of 6½"-wide border strips around the perimeter. Consult the size chart on page 20.

Cut it out

Using your rotary cutter, ruler, and mat, cut out pieces of your prewashed solid fabric according to the cutting guide. Cut out the largest pieces first.

Mix it up

Position each piece on your design wall according to the pattern diagram. Using the Scraphazard Quilt Design technique described on page 20, replace several solid fabric pieces with print pieces in the corresponding color. Audition a mix of print fabrics by cutting out pieces one by one and swapping them in and out until you've reached a lively balance of plain and patterned. Take your time and enjoy this process!

Piece the blocks

Although this clock looks like a housetop design (page 92) with its concentric squares, its construction follows a log cabin piecing sequence (page 89). Here, strips are pieced in turn off a central square or rectangle that sits in the corner of each block.

1. Starting with BLOCK 1, arrange the pieces as they appear in the pattern next to your sewing machine. Select the G piece in the lower right and start building off it, beginning with the G piece directly above it. Pin,

sew, and press. Next, tackle the strip above it by sewing the C piece to the D piece, and then sew that to your central unit. Now attach the F piece to the left of the unit. Continue adding strips one side at a time, pressing each seam as you go. A strip may first need 2 pieces sewn together to make the full length (as indicated by the white arrows in the diagram), but then the piecing process is the same.

Square up your block by pressing and trimming uneven edges with your rotary cutter. Reposition the block on the design wall.

Follow a similar process to piece BLOCK 2.

2. When you get to BLOCK 3, select the B piece from the lower right. For now, ignore the black clock hands, and sew on the B piece directly above the corner one. Press. Now sew on the D piece to the left of the unit. Press. Complete the central B-B-D-D-F-F formation. Now attach the clock hands. First add PIECE 2 on the bottom. Now attach PIECE 4 to the right. Continue following the log cabin sequence you've been using, adding strips one side at a time until the block is completed.

Continue working through the remaining 3 blocks using the log cabin piecing sequence and adding strips one side at a time, pressing each seam as you go.

> Piece the blocks.

Step 1

BLOCK 1

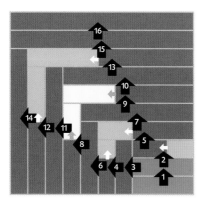

Step 2

BLOCK 3

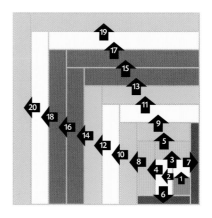

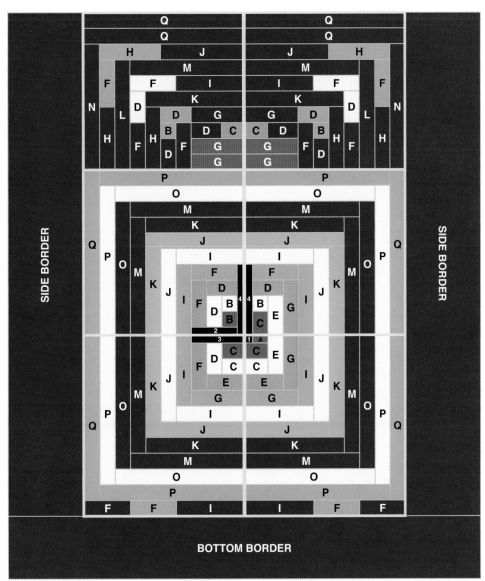

> Snooze Button pattern.

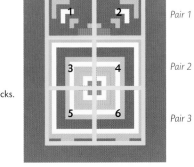

> Snooze Button blocks.

This clock has many faces

You can easily customize the look of your clock's face. Two of my favorite methods allow for an alarm clock that either seems to "snooze" a bit longer, or one that vibrates even more in the chosen design.

For a quieter clock, simplify the number of colors used in the clock face pattern. I chose to alternate colors every 2½" around the face of the clock. However, you could alternate colors every 5"—or more—to achieve wide bands of color.

For a clock that really rings out, incorporate slim bands of color by sewing 2 long strips of fabric together lengthwise and trimming the unit to the size of a pattern piece. The more color and pattern you incorporate into this design, the more dynamic the design will become.

Sew the blocks into pairs

Now that you have 6 blocks, it's time to sew them into 3 pairs. Make sure each block is thoroughly pressed. Lay BLOCK 1 on top of BLOCK 2 with right sides together. Secure the two blocks with pins, carefully pinning the seam intersections to ensure smooth transitions from strip to strip. Sew and then press.

Continue sewing the blocks together until you have 3 pairs of blocks. Pay attention to where the seams intersect to ensure smooth transitions on your clock!

Join the pairs together

Spread out the top pair and then position the middle pair on top of it, right sides together. Secure the rows with pins and sew.

Next, sew on the bottom pair of blocks. Pay attention to where the seams intersect to ensure smooth transitions.

Add borders

With right sides together, pin one of the 10½" x 64½" border strips to each side of the quilt top. Sew and press the seams toward the border.

Repeat to add the 8½" x 62½" border along the bottom of the quilt.

Finish your quilt

Hang your finished quilt top on your design wall. Stand back and admire it. Way to go! Turn to pages 29–35 for instructions on basting, quilting, and binding your quilt.

Based on: Medallion-style quilts

Medallion quilts consist of a central eye-catching panel surrounded by a series of borders of various widths. The borders can be intricately pieced or just plain fabric strips. Medallion quilts are a popular round-robin tradition in quilting groups, where each quilter adds a different border to the original maker's center square.

under lock and keys

Unlock your fabric stash to make this patchwork pleaser! This playful pattern is built up from plain ol' strips and squares and relies on daring colors and fabrics to set off its dramatic design. I chose a 1970s palette of purple, red, and chartreuse that transports me back to childhood. What colors evoke that sentimental feeling of hiding out in your old bedroom sharing secrets with your best friend? Frame your keys and lock with a cool, receding color for maximum pop, and use brash, vibrant fabrics for the keys. Such bright colors complement this highly graphic pattern. Open up the design possibilities by adding, subtracting, or using more than one color per column.

finished size:
63" x 72"

total pieces:
370

what you need:
3 yard solid dark purple fabric
1 yard solid red fabric
¾ yard solid chartreuse fabric

¾ yard solid light purple fabric
¼ yard solid light orange fabric
1½ yards assorted prints in red, chartreuse, light purple, and orange

½ yard solid purple binding fabric
4 yards backing fabric
Twin-size batting

cutting guide
Includes ¼" seam allowance

	A	B	C	D	E	F	G	H	I	J	K	L
	5½" x 4½"	2½" x 4½"	2½" x 9½"	2½" x 10½"	3" x 10½"	2½" x 2½"	2½" x 8½"	3" x 8½"	3" x 4½"	2½" x 5"	2½" x 8"	2½" x 3"
dark purple	23	30	18	–	40	33	2	13	10	6	3	1
red	–	23	14	6	–	27	2	–	–	12	–	–
chartreuse	–	14	13	5	–	12	2	–	–	–	–	–
light purple	–	16	14	6	–	14	2	–	–	–	–	–
orange	–	2	–	–	–	1	2	–	2	–	1	1

For a bigger Under Lock and Keys: Insert replicas of ROW 2 (page 81) to expand the quilt vertically and insert additional full-size blocks in each row's center to expand horizontally. Adjust the colors and arrangement as necessary. Consult the size chart on page 20.

Cut it out

Using your rotary cutter, ruler, and mat, cut out pieces of your prewashed solid fabric according to the cutting guide.

Mix it up

Position each piece on your design wall according to the pattern diagram. Using the Scraphazard Quilt Design technique described on page 20, replace several solid fabric pieces with print pieces in the corresponding color. Audition a mix of print fabrics by cutting out pieces one by one and swapping them in and out until you've reached a lively balance of plain and patterned. Take your time and enjoy this process!

Piece the blocks

Piece Under Lock and Keys one block at a time, breaking each block up into 2 units. Chain-piecing the 2 units will speed you through this process. (Illustrations, page 82)

1. Starting with BLOCK 10, arrange the pieces as they appear in the pattern next to your sewing machine. Break the key up into 2 units: the head (the part you grip when turning a key), and the body (the long part that engages the lock lever).

2. The key's head requires a simple housetop piecing strategy that builds from its center square outward. The key's body is made up of strips and squares and requires the Block Off and Buddy Up strategy described on page 26. Chain-piece these 2 units simultaneously! Starting with the head, select the center A piece and the B piece to its left. With right sides together, carefully pin and sew. Moving down to the key's body, select another pair of pieces. Pin and sew. Continue to move across the block, chain-piecing all available pairs.

   Remove the chain from your sewing machine. Press and snip the threads between the units.

3. Reposition the sewn pairs next to your sewing machine according to the pattern diagram's BLOCK 10 configuration. Now buddy up the next set of pairs. From the key's head, build onto the center A piece by sewing on the second B piece. Moving down to the key's body, select another pair of pieces. Continue to move across the block, chain-piecing all available pairs. Press.

4. Perform 3 more rounds of buddying up, chain-piecing, and pressing until the block is completed.

   Square up your block by pressing and trimming uneven edges with your rotary cutter. Reposition the block on the design wall.

   When you are ready, tackle the remaining key blocks. The keys along the edges are modified with fewer pieces but can be broken up into 2 units and pieced much like the full-size key blocks.

5. When you get to the lock in BLOCK 31, break the block up into units that square off. Using the Block Off and Buddy Up strategy, perform several rounds of buddying up, chain-piecing, and pressing until the block is completed.

Based on:
Strips and squares

Sewing strips of fabric together is possibly one of the easiest ways to piece a quilt! Add in the old reliable square, and the design possibilities are endless. Quilters throughout the ages have relied on these two most basic straight-sided shapes to make simple and effective patchwork artistry.

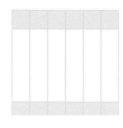

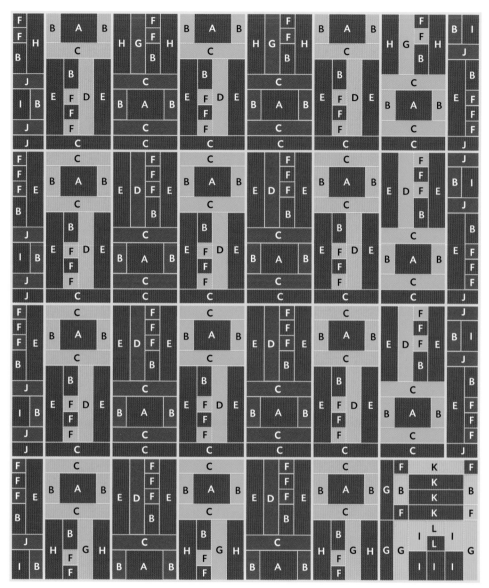

> Under Lock and Keys pattern.

> Under Lock and Keys blocks.

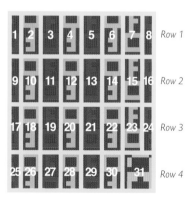

> Piece the blocks.

Step 1

BLOCK 10

Step 2

Round 1

Step 3

Round 2

Step 4

Round 3

Round 4

Round 5

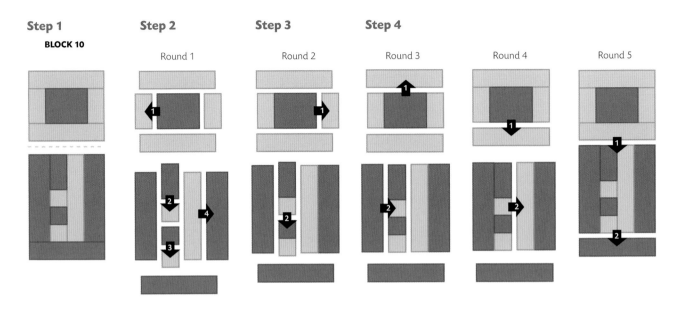

Step 5

BLOCK 31

Round 1

Round 2

Round 3

Round 4

Round 5

Sew the blocks into rows

Make sure each block is thoroughly pressed. Lay BLOCK 1 on top of BLOCK 2 with right sides together. Secure the 2 blocks with pins. Sew and press. Next, sew BLOCK 3 to 4, BLOCK 5 to 6, and BLOCK 7 to 8. Now sew these joined blocks together into a row.

Continue sewing the blocks together until you have 4 rows of 8 blocks each (ROW 4 contains 7 blocks because the lock block is wider than the others).

Join the rows together

It's more manageable to first join the rows into 2 groups. Over a long table, spread out ROW 1 and then position ROW 2 on top of it, right sides together. Carefully align the seams. Secure the rows with pins and sew.

Next, sew ROW 3 to 4. Now join the 2 groups. Be sure to press the seams as you go.

Finish your quilt

Hang your finished quilt top on your design wall. Turn to pages 29–35 for instructions on basting, quilting, and binding your quilt.

hootenanny

You may become nocturnal making this quilt—it's so much fun to design you won't sleep 'til it's done! Rich dark brown frames the owl, letting this bold bird's plumage take center stage. I chose a retro palette of analogous greens and blues, but any bright color combination will flatter this distinguished creature. For best results, alternate light and dark values within the owl's log cabin formations, and follow the perpendicular paths of the logs across the blocks. Get out your "star players"—this quilt is a prime place to showcase those personality-packed fabrics.

finished size:	what you need:		
60" x 72½"	3¼ yards solid dark brown fabric	1 yard solid green fabrics in olives, khakis, and yellow-greens	½ yard solid dark brown binding fabric
total pieces:	1 yard solid blue fabrics in teals, turquoises, and light blues	1½ yards assorted prints in greens, blues, and additional accents	4 yards backing fabric
192			Twin-size batting

cutting guide
Includes ¼" seam allowance

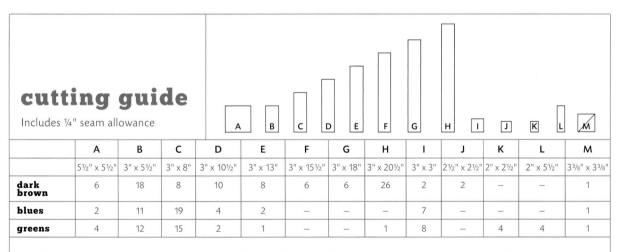

	A	B	C	D	E	F	G	H	I	J	K	L	M
	5½" x 5½"	3" x 5½"	3" x 8"	3" x 10½"	3" x 13"	3" x 15½"	3" x 18"	3" x 20½"	3" x 3"	2½" x 2½"	2" x 2½"	2" x 5½"	3⅜" x 3⅜"
dark brown	6	18	8	10	8	6	6	26	2	2	–	–	1
blues	2	11	19	4	2	–	–	–	7	–	–	–	1
greens	4	12	15	2	1	–	–	1	8	–	4	4	1

For a bigger Hootenanny: Add one or more sets of 6½"-wide border strips around the perimeter. Consult the size chart on page 20.

Cut it out

Using your rotary cutter, ruler, and mat, cut out pieces of your prewashed solid fabric according to the cutting guide. Cut the square M pieces in half diagonally to form the triangle pieces for the owl's beak.

Mix it up

Position each piece on your design wall according to the pattern diagram. Using the Scraphazard Quilt Design technique described on page 20, replace several solid fabric pieces with print pieces in the corresponding color. Audition a mix of print fabrics by cutting out pieces one by one and swapping them in and out until you've reached a lively balance of plain and patterned. Take your time and enjoy this process!

Piece the blocks

This pattern loosely follows a log cabin piecing sequence. The large A pieces form the anchors of the blocks you will assemble. Strips are pieced from the A piece outward to build up the design. Take note that the owl's beak is composed of the only 3-sided shapes in this entire book—so here's your chance to try working with triangles.

1. Starting with BLOCK 1, arrange the pieces as they appear in the pattern next to your sewing machine. Select the A piece in the lower right and start building off it, beginning with the B piece. Pin, sew, and press. Next, sew on the innermost C piece. Continue adding strips one side at a time, pressing each seam as you go. A strip may first need 2 or 3 pieces sewn together to make the full length (as indicated by the white arrows in the diagram), but then the piecing process is the same.

   Square up your block by pressing and trimming uneven edges with your rotary cutter. You've got a completed block! Position the block on the design wall.

2. Follow a similar process for BLOCK 2. BLOCK 2 has two A pieces that serve as the log cabin centers, so build off each of them until their strips collide. Speed up the process by chain-piecing the pieces, working the two A-B-C-C-D formations simultaneously.

   Piece BLOCKS 3 and 4 using a similar process.

3. When you get to BLOCK 5, select the J-K-L formations that comprise the owl's 2 eyes. Starting with a J piece, sew K pieces to its top and bottom. Press. Now sew L pieces to its two sides. Press. After doing this with both J-K-L sets, you have two honorary A pieces to build

> Piece the blocks.

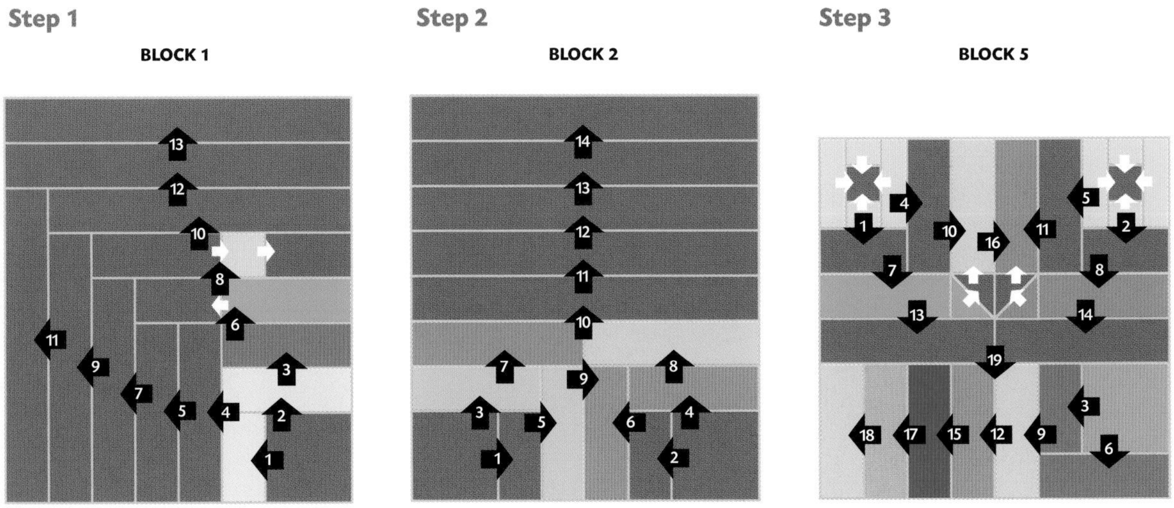

Step 1

BLOCK 1

Step 2

BLOCK 2

Step 3

BLOCK 5

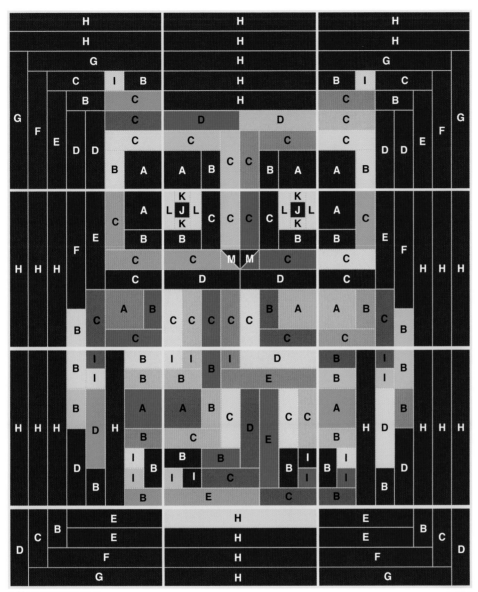

> Hootenanny pattern.

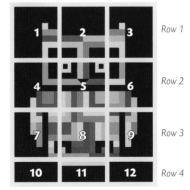

> Hootenanny blocks.

upon, as well as one real A piece. Follow the log cabin piecing sequence you've been using in BLOCKS 1–4. You'll need to sew the 2 sets of M piece triangles together into squares and join them to strips, but otherwise the piecing process is the same.

Follow a similar log cabin piecing sequence for BLOCK 6.

4. When you get to BLOCK 7, you'll see that the log cabin piecing sequence cannot be used. Instead, break the block up into units that square off. Using the Block Off and Buddy Up strategy on page 26, perform 5 rounds of buddying up, chain-piecing, and pressing until the block is completed.

Continue working through the remaining 5 blocks, either piecing log cabin formations in sequence or employing the Block Off and Buddy Up strategy where necessary.

Sew the blocks into rows

Now that you have 12 blocks, it's time to sew them into 4 rows. Make sure each block is thoroughly pressed. Starting with ROW 1, lay BLOCK 1 on top of BLOCK 2 with right sides together. Secure the two blocks with pins, paying special attention to the seam intersections to ensure smooth edges on the owl. Sew and then press. Then sew BLOCK 3 to BLOCK 2.

Continue sewing the blocks together until you have 4

Step 4

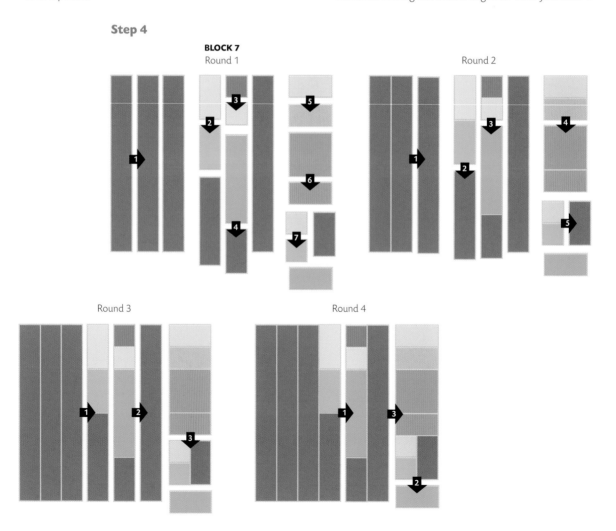

rows of 3 blocks each. Pay attention to where the brown fabric's seams intersect to ensure smooth transitions on your owl.

Join the rows together

It's time to sew those rows into one giant quilt top. It's more manageable to first join the rows into 2 groups. Over a long table, spread out ROW 1 and then position ROW 2 on top of it, right sides together. Carefully align the seams. Secure the rows with pins. Now take a deep breath and sew. Next, sew ROW 3 to 4. Now join the 2 groups. Be sure to press those seams as you go.

Finish your quilt

Hang your finished quilt top on your design wall. Stand back and admire it. Way to go! Turn to pages 29–35 for instructions on basting, quilting, and binding your quilt.

Based on:
Log cabin

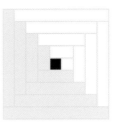

A traditional log cabin block is constructed from the middle outward, with fabric strips sewn in sequence around the sides of a center square. The center is typically red, symbolizing the hearth of a home. The block is separated into two triangles of color, with light fabrics on one half and darks on the other. This light and dark contrast represents the effects of sunshine and shadow on a house. A secondary pattern emerges depending on how you arrange the finished blocks.

blockheads

These silly, smiling Blockheads are guaranteed to cure the blahs and make for the happiest housetop quilt I've ever seen! You can either zigzag-stitch these happy line-drawn faces, or create your very own quadrilateral style. High-contrast black and white, along with complementary blue and orange, give these squares eye-popping impact. See, it's true: Opposites really do attract! Use prints sparingly to preserve the highly graphic, mod feeling of these housetop clusters (I chose a single black plaid that looks like a solid but adds texture up close). Keep the art in the center squares bold and simple with a minimum of colors that read clearly from a distance. How will you infuse personality into these twenty-nine blockheads?

finished size:	what you need:		for the faces you will
63" x 72"	1¾ yards solid black fabric	½ yard solid orange binding	need:
	1⅜ yards solid orange fabric	fabric	Tear-away stabilizer
total pieces:	1¼ yards solid blue fabric	4 yards backing fabric	Fabric adhesive spray
145	¾ yard solid white fabric	Twin-size batting	Liquid seam sealant, such as
	¼ yard assorted prints in black		Fray-Check
	or orange		Machine embroidery thread

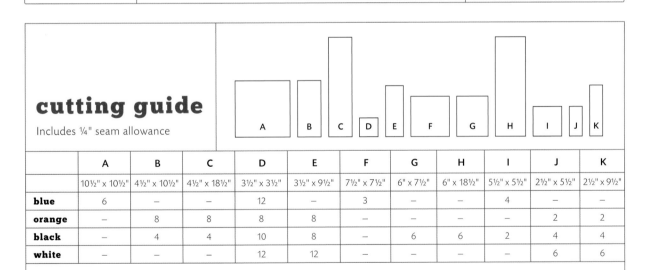

cutting guide

Includes ¼" seam allowance

	A	B	C	D	E	F	G	H	I	J	K
	10½" x 10½"	4½" x 10½"	4½" x 18½"	3½" x 3½"	3½" x 9½"	7½" x 7½"	6" x 7½"	6" x 18½"	5½" x 5½"	2½" x 5½"	2½" x 9½"
blue	6	–	–	12	–	3	–	–	4	–	–
orange	–	8	8	8	8	–	–	–	–	2	2
black	–	4	4	10	8	–	6	6	2	4	4
white	–	–	–	12	12	–	–	–	–	6	6

For a bigger Blockheads: Add blocks to the side and bottom, repeating BLOCK 1 for an extra 18" or BLOCK 2 for an extra 9" where needed (page 93). Adjust the colors as necessary. Consult the size chart on page 20.

Cut it out

Using your rotary cutter, ruler, and mat, cut out pieces of your prewashed solid fabric according to the cutting guide.

Mix it up

Position each piece on your design wall according to the pattern diagram. Using the Scraphazard Quilt Design technique described on page 20, replace several solid fabric pieces with print pieces in the corresponding color. Audition a mix of print fabrics by cutting out pieces one by one and swapping them in and out until you've reached a lively balance of plain and patterned. Take your time and enjoy this process!

Create the art for each block's center square. See Smile Ear-to-Ear with Side-to-Side Stitching on page 94 for instructions.

Piece the blocks

Blockheads follows a super simple housetop piecing sequence. Strips are pieced in turn outward from each block's center square. Minimal seam intersections make this quilt a snap to stitch!

1. Starting with BLOCK 1, arrange the pieces as they appear in the pattern next to your sewing machine. Select the middle A and build off it, beginning with the B piece to its left. Pin, sew, and press. Next, attach the B piece to the right. Now attach the C pieces to the top and bottom.

    Square up your block by pressing and trimming uneven edges with your rotary cutter. You've got a completed block! Position the block on the design wall.

    Follow a similar process for BLOCKS 2 and 3. Continue working through the remaining 26 blocks, using the housetop piecing sequence and adding strips one side at a time, pressing each seam as you go.

Sew the blocks into groups

Now that you have 29 blocks, it's time to sew them into 4 groups. Make sure each block is thoroughly pressed. Starting with GROUP 1, first sew the smaller blocks into larger units using the Block Off and Buddy Up strategy described on page 26. Next, working from left to right, sew each block or unit to the one next to it. Press those seams as you go.

When you are ready, tackle the remaining 3 groups. First sew the smaller blocks into larger units, and then work from top to bottom by sewing each block or unit to the one next to it. Press those seams as you go.

[Tip] *Want to give your Blockheads quilt its own distinct personality? Get experimental with fabric paint and stencils, fabric markers, or ink-jet transfers. For recommended reading on these techniques, visit the Resources section on page 157. Or make this quilt a group project! Assign the art for the small, medium, and large squares randomly to friends or family members. Even the tiny squares can contain big ideas!*

Based on: Housetop

A simple housetop block looks like squares within squares. This popular block is constructed from the middle outward, with fabric strips sewn in sequence around the sides of a center piece. Typically, each strip set  alternates between light and dark. The concentric squares of a housetop block represent the elevation of the roof of a house seen from above.

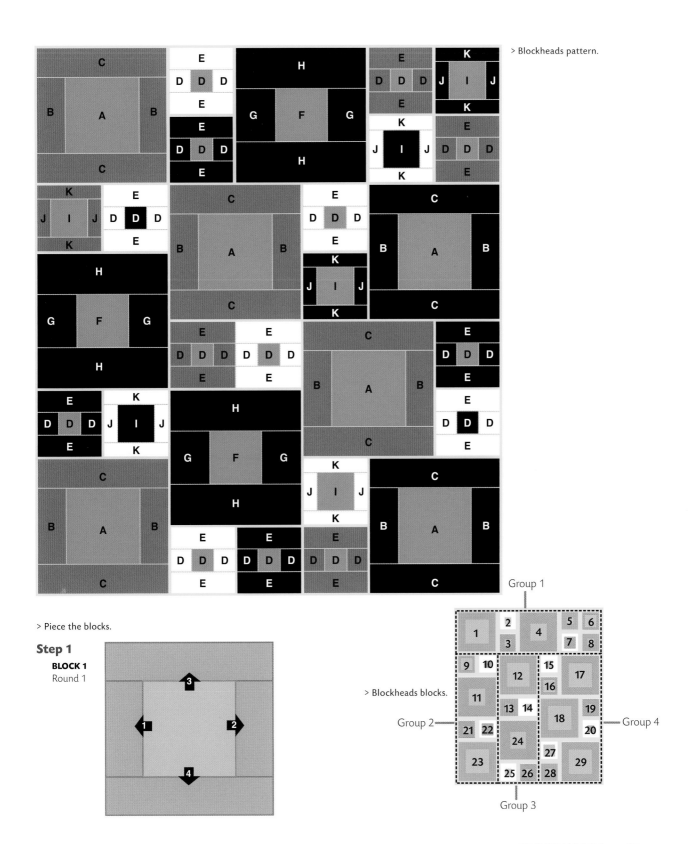

> Blockheads pattern.

> Blockheads blocks.

Group 1

Group 2

Group 4

Group 3

> Piece the blocks.

Step 1

BLOCK 1
Round 1

Join the groups together

It's time to sew those groups into one giant quilt top. Over a long table, spread out GROUP 2 and then position GROUP 3 on top of it, right sides together. Pay attention to where the seams intersect. Secure the groups with pins. Now take a deep breath, sew, and press.

Next, sew on GROUP 4. Press. Finally attach GROUP 1. Press.

Finish your quilt

Hang your finished quilt top on your design wall. Stand back and admire it. Way to go! Turn to pages 29–35 for instructions on basting, quilting, and binding your quilt.

Smile ear-to-ear with side-to-side stitching

If you like the look of machine-stitched smiling faces, use the zigzag stitch on your home sewing machine to simulate professional machine embroidery!

Using scrap fabric, experiment with a tight zigzag at various angles and try pivoting on a curve. Use an embroidery foot if you have one, which allows you to see the fabric more easily. When you've practiced this technique and feel comfortable zigzagging on a curve, follow these steps:

PREPARE YOUR BLOCKS

Freehand a smiley face onto your fabric square with a quilt pencil, or trace a face from the templates on page 155. Use a quilt pencil to trace the face onto each fabric square. Add some variety by flipping the image horizontally for some blocks to get a mirror image of the face.

Use a fabric adhesive spray to affix tear-away embroidery stabilizer to the back of your fabric square. The stabilizer doesn't need to cover the entire back of the square, just the area behind the image of the face. This will give your fabric added stability and help prevent puckering.

SEW YOUR DESIGN

Using machine embroidery thread, stitch on the right side of the fabric, following the lines of the quilt pencil. Use a wide 5mm stitch width for the larger faces, a 4mm stitch for the medium-sized faces, and a narrow 3mm stitch for the smaller ones. Alternate black and white thread from face to face. Take your time, and don't rush this process.

When you have finished sewing a face, turn the square over and secure your stitching by applying seam sealant to the starts and stops of your zigzags. Tear away the embroidery stabilizer after the sealant has dried. Press the square thoroughly from the back.

Repeat this process for a total of 29 faces. You may want to sew several extra faces so you can choose your favorites.

If you are short on time or patience, have an embroidery professional digitize the smiling faces and machine-stitch them for you! Go to your local sewing machine shop and ask the quilting professionals to recommend a reliable embroiderer. Then, contact the savvy stitcher to discuss your project's specs. Ask what types of digital file formats are preferred and the necessary resolution before scanning the faces on page 155. Organize your digital files and fabric squares, and drop them off to be completed. You'll be ready to piece the blocks in no time!

PART 3:
Patchwork Projects

Quilts are great, but you can't take them to the grocery store! Never fear, I offer you a bounty of more portable projects that add scrap-happiness to all areas of your life. From totes to table runners, these simple but sturdy projects are long on charm but short on time required to make them. All of these qualify as easy starter projects or something an experienced seamster can whip up on a lazy Sunday afternoon. The "Straight-Up Sewing" projects in this section are simple-to-stitch designs that look patchworky, but aren't. Don't worry, you'll have plenty of chances to perfect your piecing technique with the pillows and other "Patchworkin' It" projects. From there, the "Hey, You're Quilting" projects require all of the skills of quilt-making but none of the patience. Besides brightening your daily routine, these projects give you the opportunity to go nuts with color and fabric. So go on, get scrappy!

all in a flap book cover

Go ahead and judge these books by their covers. These guys are up for the challenge. Practical, pretty, and simple to sew, oilcloth is a printed vinyl with a cotton mesh backside (that means its raw edges won't unravel or fray). These durable and waterproof covers can be wiped clean, which makes them perfect for covering *Introduction to Earth Science* or other texts that may take a beating. Since oilcloth comes in dozens of vintage-inspired designs in super-saturated palettes—vibrant fruits, florals, and ginghams are typical oilcloth motifs—pair one or two attention-grabbing prints with calmer solids, polka dots, and stripes. Your stylishly protected book will thank you.

level of difficulty:
Straight-Up Sewing

finished size:
Sized to fit any book

total pieces:
2

what you need:
Oilcloth in 2 coordinating prints or solids, enough to cover the book of your choice
A book to cover

Measure and cut

An All in a Flap Book Cover is made up of just two pieces: a main A piece that covers the book, and the accent B piece that folds over the spine. Because oilcloth retains a clean edge when cut, there are no frayed, raw edges to conceal—so pieces can be sewn directly on top of each other. This is patchwork goodness minus the seams!

Cut out the A and B pieces from two different styles of oilcloth. Test-drive your cuts by loosely wrapping them around your book. There should be enough excess fabric along the top and bottom to accommodate stitching the flaps closed ⅛" from the edge, with a bit of "sliding room" between the book's edge and stitching. Also, see if you like where the B piece lands on the front and back covers when wrapped around the spine. Trim off excess oilcloth as necessary.

Sew it up

1. With right sides up, center the B piece along the width of the A piece. Pin in place. (Use as few pins as possible; oilcloth will retain small holes when pins are removed. If tiny holes bother you, try using paper clips instead of pins.) Stitch along each side of the B piece's length, ⅛" from the inside edge.

    Wrap the cover snugly around your book, folding the fabric evenly over the front and back covers to make flaps. Make a crease at both folds. Remove the cover from the book, and pin the flaps at the creases.

2. Stitch the flaps to the cover. With your cover wrong side up, stitch ⅛" from the top edge, over each flap. Back-stitch at the beginning and end to secure your thread. Next stitch ⅛" from the bottom edge, over each flap, backstitching at the beginning and end.

Slide your book's front cover into the front flap. To get your book's back cover into your new creation, you'll have to gently bend the book's back cover backward away from the spine to slide it into place.

Step 1

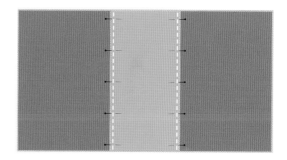

Step 2

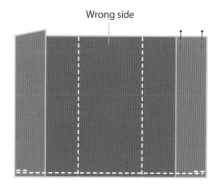

Wrong side

[Tip] *For a book cover that will be getting lots of wear and tear, add an additional line of stitching along the top and bottom for extra reinforcement.*

peek-a-boo patchwork scarf

There's no good reason to abandon fun florals or bouncy dots just because the temperature takes a dive. This patchwork wrap alternates a sunny, printed cotton with a heavy-textured fuzzy find for a graphic peek-a-boo effect. Pick a print that'll remind you of spring when you need it—here I harnessed some flower power to peek out through dark brown faux wool. While I chose a sedate two-fabric combo, you can mix in additional cotton prints for a scrappier scarf. Choose a fun coordinating or contrasting thread for the topstitching—here, pink stitching adds pop. For a longer scarf, add more strips and increase the length of the border strips.

level of difficulty:	what you need:
Patchworkin' it	½ yard wool-like brown solid fabric
	¼ yard cotton pink print fabric
finished size:	½ yard dark pink flannel backing fabric
60" x 6"	
total pieces:	
37 plus 2 border strips	

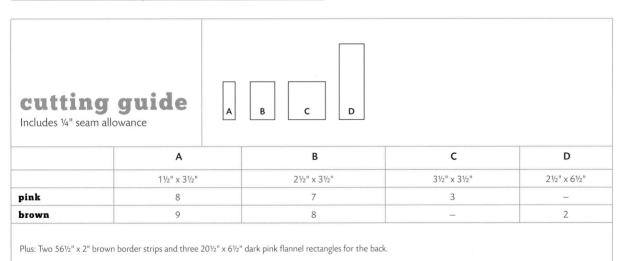

cutting guide
Includes ¼" seam allowance

	A	B	C	D
	1½" x 3½"	2½" x 3½"	3½" x 3½"	2½" x 6½"
pink	8	7	3	–
brown	9	8	–	2

Plus: Two 56½" x 2" brown border strips and three 20½" x 6½" dark pink flannel rectangles for the back.

Cut it out

Using your rotary cutter, ruler, and mat, cut out pieces of your fabric according to the cutting guide.

Position each piece on your design wall (or some other flat surface) according to the pattern diagram. If necessary, audition different fabrics until you find a design you are happy with.

Piece the scarf front

Piece the scarf in 3 sections. Arrange the pieces for SECTION 1 as they appear in the pattern next to your sewing machine. Buddy up the pieces into pairs.

1. Working from left to right, select the first pair. Pin and sew. Don't cut the thread or lift the presser foot just yet! Next, select the next pair and sew it to the chain. Continue to chain-piece the remaining pairs in the section.

   Remove the chain from your sewing machine. Press seams toward the darker pieces and cut the threads between the units.

2. Reposition the sewn pairs next to your sewing machine according to the pattern's SECTION 1 configuration. On to the next round! Working from left to right, buddy up and chain-piece the joined pairs. Press seams toward the darker fabric. Continue sewing the strips and pressing until you have a completed section.

   Square up your joined section by pressing and trimming uneven edges with your rotary cutter.

   Repeat for the remaining 2 sections.

   Sew the 3 sections together.

3. Add decorative topstitching on each of the darker strips. Using hot pink thread, sew ⅛" from the seams over the seam allowance.

Add borders

You may need to piece these border strips to get the proper length. With right sides together, pin one of the 56½" x 2" brown border strips to each side of the scarf. Sew and press the seams toward the border. Next, sew on the D pieces to each end, pressing seams toward the ends of the scarf.

4. Add decorative topstitching in a rectangle around the center strips. Sew ⅛" from the inside seam (over the seam allowance) of the border strips and the D pieces, backstitching at the beginning and the end of the seam to secure the stitches.

Stitch the scarf back

Sew together the short ends of the three 20½" x 6½" dark pink flannel rectangles for the back. Press. Add decorative topstitching ⅛" from the seams over the seam allowance.

Sew the scarf front and back together

5. With right sides together, position the scarf back on top of the scarf front. Align the edges and pin in place.

   Stitch around the perimeter of the scarf through both layers with a ¼" seam allowance, pivoting at each corner. Leave a 5" opening at the center bottom, backstitching at the beginning and the end of the seam to secure the stitches. Press flat and trim the corners.

   Turn the scarf right side out through the opening, gently pushing out the corners into points with your finger. Fold in the seam allowance at the 5" opening. Press flat.

6. Add decorative topstitching ¼" inside the perimeter of the scarf, making sure to stitch over the seam allowance of the 5" opening to close it.

Step 1

Step 2

> Peek-A-Boo Patchwork Scarf pattern.

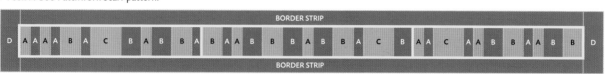

> Piece the scarf front.

Step 3

> Add borders.

Step 4

> Sew the front and back together.

Step 5

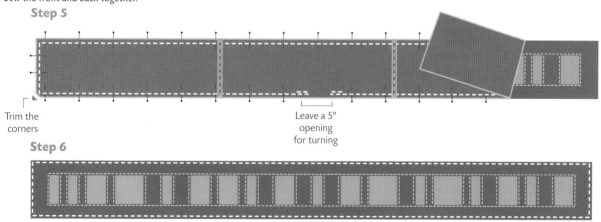

Trim the corners

Leave a 5" opening for turning

Step 6

Tuck in seam and topstitch

op art floor pillow

This optical illusion pillow will make you look twice before settling in to its receding housetop design. Concentric squares, a simple color scheme, and a generously sized pillow are all you need to trick the eye and turn your floor into the best seat in the house. Solid, groovy greens play nice with this trick-of-the-eye design. Picking a deep bold main color will help the shyer shade recede and make the illusion a lofty success. Add a little pop with a square of something unexpected right at the center—here it's a bright chartreuse. Whatever your palette, this pillow is an op-art masterpiece . . . or at least an extra chair in a pinch.

level of difficulty:
Patchworkin' It

finished size:
27" x 27"

total pieces:
45 plus 2 back pieces

what you need:
½ yard solid dark green fabric
½ yard solid light green fabric
⅛ yard solid chartreuse green fabric
1 yard solid chartreuse backing fabric
27" x 27" pillow form

cutting guide
Includes ¼" seam allowance

		dark green	light green	chartreuse
A	1½" x 1½"	–	1	–
B	1" x 1½"	2	–	–
C	1" x 2½"	2	2	–
D	1" x 3½"	2	2	–
E	1" x 4½"	2	–	–
F	1¼" x 4½"	–	–	2
G	1¼" x 6"	2	–	2
H	1¼" x 7½"	2	–	–
I	1½" x 7½"	–	2	–
J	1½" x 9½"	–	2	–
K	1¾" x 9½"	2	–	–
L	1¾" x 12"	2	2	–
M	1¾" x 14½"	–	2	–
N	2¼" x 14½"	2	–	–
O	2¼" x 18"	2	–	–
P	2½" x 18"	–	2	–
Q	2½" x 22"	–	2	–
R	3½" x 22"	2	–	–
S	3½" x 28"	2	–	–

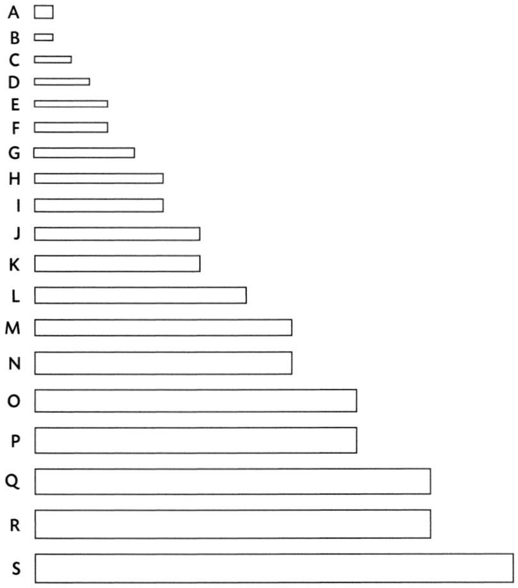

A
B
C
D
E
F
G
H
I
J
K
L
M
N
O
P
Q
R
S

Plus: Two 28" x 18" pieces of fabric.

Cut it out

Using your rotary cutter, ruler, and mat, cut out pieces of your prewashed solid fabric according to the cutting guide.

Mix it up

Position each piece on your design wall (or some other flat surface) according to the pattern diagram.

Piece the pillow front

The Op Art Floor Pillow follows a housetop piecing sequence (page 92). Strips are pieced in turn outward from the center A square.

1. Arrange the pieces as they appear in the pattern next to your sewing machine. Select the middle A square and build off it, beginning with the B piece above it. Pin, sew, and press. Next, sew on the B piece below it. Press. Now attach the C pieces to each side. Continue to build outward through the remaining pieces.

   Square up your pillow front to 28" x 28" by pressing and trimming uneven edges with your rotary cutter.

Attach the pillow back

2. Double-turn a ½" hem by folding the edge over twice on one long side of each of the 28" x 18" pieces of chartreuse fabric. Stitch ⅛" from the inside edge of the hem.

3. With right sides together, lay one pillow back on top of the pillow front, with raw edges aligned and the ½" hem in the center. Pin in place. With right side down, position the second pillow back on top, with the raw edges aligned and the ½" hem facing the center. Stitch around the perimeter using a ½" seam allowance. Press. Trim the corners.

   Turn the pillow cover right side out through the opening between the back pieces, using your finger to push out the corners. Press flat. Insert your pillow form.

> Piece the pillow front.

Step 1

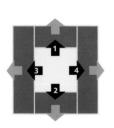

> Attach the pillow back.

Step 2

Double-turn a ½" hem

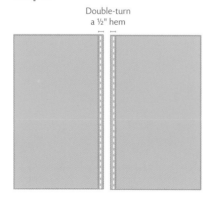

Step 3

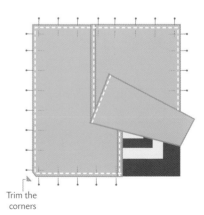

Trim the corners

> Op Art Floor Pillow pattern.

bright lights, patchwork city pillow

Are you a city mouse? Do you love the sound of cars driving by and find comfort in having a dozen coffee shops all within walking distance? This low and lovely bolster pillow brings a bustling neighborhood right to your sofa. The design here shines best when made with just a few bold solids and one coordinating print. You can't beat the graphic impact of black and white, along with bright blue and red. Choose a quartet of colors that contrast in a similar way (I chose a low-key black polka-dot print to add texture to an otherwise stark skyline). Be selective and make each color count!

level of difficulty:	total pieces:	what you need:	
Patchworkin' It	120 plus 2 back pieces	¼ yard solid black fabric	¼ yard black print fabric
		¼ yard solid white fabric	½ yard solid white backing
finished size:		¼ yard solid red fabric	fabric
28" x 14"		¼ yard solid blue fabric	28" x 14" pillow form

cutting guide
Includes ¼" seam allowance

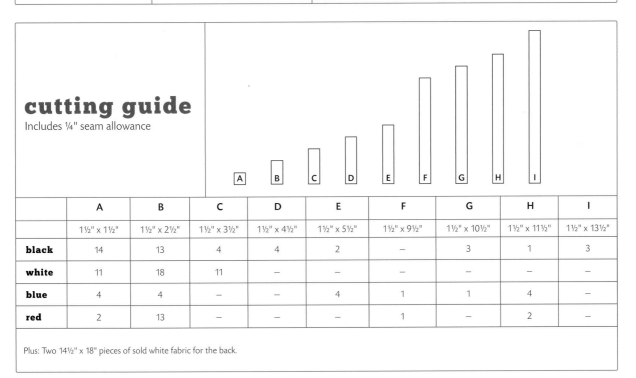

	A	B	C	D	E	F	G	H	I
	1½" x 1½"	1½" x 2½"	1½" x 3½"	1½" x 4½"	1½" x 5½"	1½" x 9½"	1½" x 10½"	1½" x 11½"	1½" x 13½"
black	14	13	4	4	2	–	3	1	3
white	11	18	11	–	–	–	–	–	–
blue	4	4	–	–	4	1	1	4	–
red	2	13	–	–	–	1	–	2	–

Plus: Two 14½" x 18" pieces of sold white fabric for the back.

Cut it out

Using your rotary cutter, ruler, and mat, cut out pieces of your prewashed fabric according to the cutting guide.

Mix it up

Position each piece on your design wall (or some other flat surface) according to the pattern diagram. If necessary, audition different fabrics until you find a design you are happy with.

Piece the pillow front

The Bright Lights, Patchwork City Pillow is built entirely from strips. Construct this cityscape building by building, buddying up and chain-piecing from strip to strip.

1. Arrange the pieces for BUILDING 1 as they appear in the pattern next to your sewing machine. Divide the building up into 4 vertical strips.

2. From the first strip on the left, buddy up the top 2 A pieces. Pin and sew. Don't cut the thread or lift the presser foot just yet! Next buddy up the pair directly

below it, sewing it on to the chain. Continue moving from top to bottom and then move to the next strip to the right, buddying up all available pairs in each strip and sewing them on to the chain.

Remove the chain from your sewing machine. Press and snip the threads between the pairs.

3. Reposition the sewn pairs next to your sewing machine according to the pattern's BUILDING 1 configuration. On to the next round! From the first strip on the left, buddy up the top 2 joined pairs. Pin and sew. Don't cut the thread or lift the presser foot just yet! Next buddy up the joined pairs directly below it, sewing it on to the chain. Continue moving from top to bottom and then strip to strip, buddying up all available pairs and sewing them on to the chain. Press.

4. Sew the 4 strips together.

Repeat the piecing process for the remaining 5 buildings. Four of the buildings are made up of 5 strips, but the process is the same.

> Piece the pillow front.

Step 1

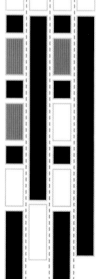

Step 2

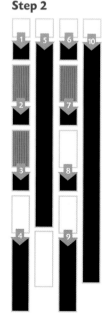

Step 3

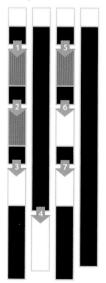

Step 4

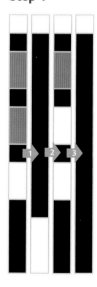

> Bright Lights, Patchwork City Pillow pattern.

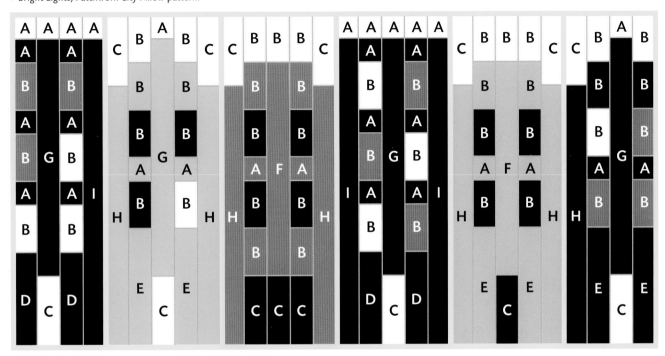

> Bright Lights, Patchwork City Pillow buildings.

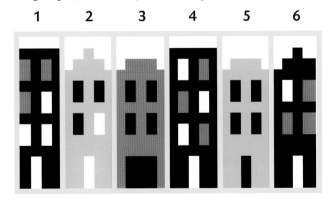

1   2   3   4   5   6

Sew the buildings

Sew together the 6 buildings.

Square up your pillow front to 28½" x 14½" by pressing and trimming uneven edges with your rotary cutter.

Attach the pillow back

5. Double-turn a ½" hem by folding the edge over twice on one short side of each of the 14½" x 18" pieces of white fabric. Stitch ⅛" from the inside edge of the hem.

6. With right sides together, lay one pillow back on top of the pillow front, with raw edges aligned and the ½" hem in the center. Pin in place.

With right side down, position the second pillow back on top, with the raw edges aligned and the ½" hem facing the center. Stitch around the perimeter using a ¼" seam allowance. Press. Trim the corners.

Turn the pillow cover right side out through the opening between the back pieces, using your finger to push out the corners. Press flat. Insert your pillow form.

> Attach the pillow back.

Step 5

Double-turn
a ½" hem

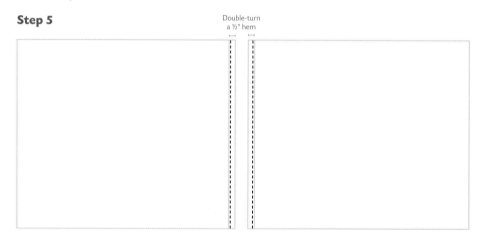

Step 6

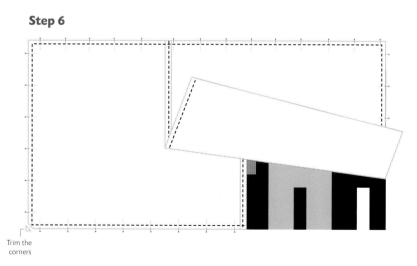

Trim the
corners

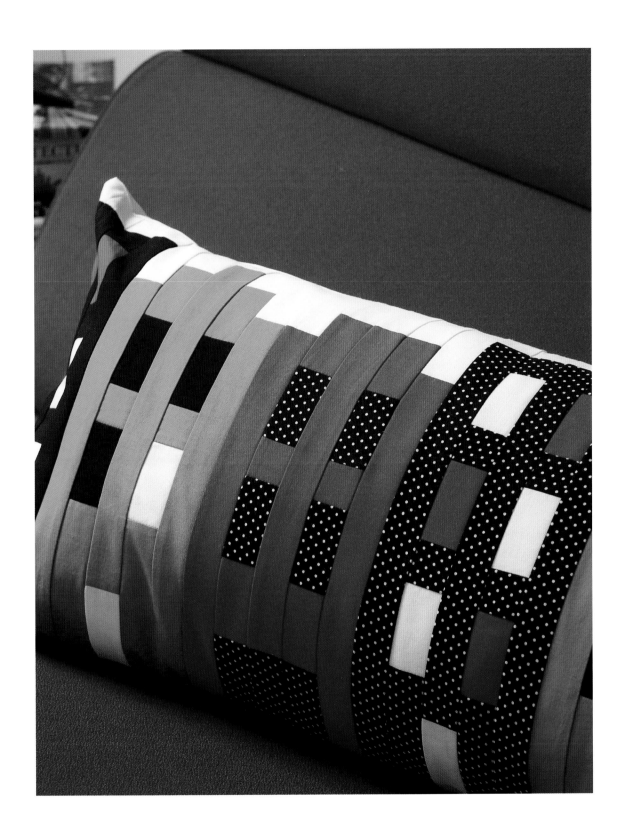

chain reaction table runner

Table runner by day and backup trivet by dinnertime, this versatile quilted table topper never misses a meal. Add a snappy solid fabric around a chain of off-white to frame your favorite personality-packed prints. I chose retro-hued blues and browns that mingle with outrageous orange to create a color palette comfortable in my mildly mid-century home. Feel free to shabby yours up with soft pinks and faded florals. Modern more your thing? Sticking to striking solids should do the trick. If necessary, add or subtract the housetop blocks to make a runner that fits your table.

level of difficulty:
Hey, You're Quilting!

finished size:
72" x 18"

total pieces:
59 plus 2 border strips

what you need:
2⅛ yards solid blue fabric
½ yard cream solid or print fabric
¼ yard orange print fabric
¼ yard brown print fabric

⅓ yard solid blue binding fabric
2¼ yards backing fabric
2¼ yards batting

cutting guide
Includes ¼" seam allowance

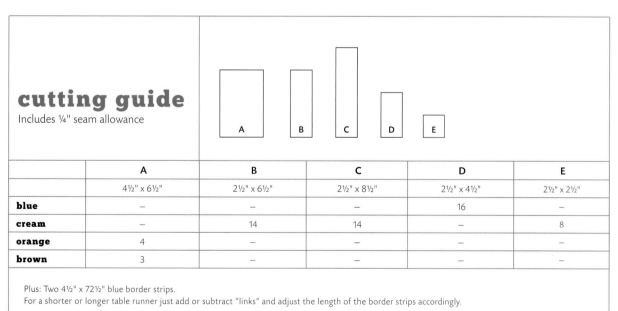

	A	B	C	D	E
	4½" x 6½"	2½" x 6½"	2½" x 8½"	2½" x 4½"	2½" x 2½"
blue	–	–	–	16	–
cream	–	14	14	–	8
orange	4	–	–	–	–
brown	3	–	–	–	–

Plus: Two 4½" x 72½" blue border strips.
For a shorter or longer table runner just add or subtract "links" and adjust the length of the border strips accordingly.

Cut it out

Using your rotary cutter, ruler, and mat, cut out pieces of your prewashed solid fabric according to the cutting guide.

Mix it up

Position each piece on your design wall (or some other flat surface) according to the pattern diagram. If necessary, audition different fabrics by cutting out pieces one by one and swapping them in and out until you find a design you are happy with.

Piece the blocks

Piece the table runner one block at a time. Each block contains both a 3-piece strip and a simple housetop configuration (page 92). In a housetop piecing sequence, strips are pieced in turn outward from the center A pieces. Chain-piece the block's strip and housetop configurations simultaneously.

Arrange the pieces for BLOCK 1 as they appear in the pattern next to your sewing machine.

1. Select a D and E piece from the top strip. Pin and sew. Without cutting the thread or lifting the presser foot, move over to the housetop formation. Buddy up the A piece and the B piece above it. Pin and sew. For more on this Block Off and Buddy Up approach, turn to page 26.
    Remove the chain from your sewing machine. Press and cut the threads between the units.

2. Reposition the sewn pairs next to your sewing machine according to the pattern diagram. On to the next round! Finish the strip by sewing on the second D piece. Without cutting the thread or lifting the presser foot, move over to the housetop formation. Buddy up the A piece and the B piece below it. Pin, sew, and press.

3. Complete the housetop configuration by sewing on the side C pieces.

4. Finish the block by sewing the strip to the completed housetop unit.
    Square up your block by pressing and trimming uneven edges with your rotary cutter.

Repeat the piecing process for the remaining 6 blocks. BLOCK 7 contains an extra strip that can be pieced and sewn on last.

Sew the blocks

Now that you have 7 blocks, it's time to sew them into one row. Make sure each block is thoroughly pressed. Starting with BLOCK 1, lay it on top of BLOCK 2 with right sides together. Secure the 2 blocks with pins and sew. Buddy up the blocks and sew. Continue sewing together all 7 blocks.

Add borders

With right sides together, pin one of the 4½" x 72½" border strips to each side of the table runner. Sew and press the seams toward the border.

Baste, quilt, and bind

Handle this table runner exactly like a mini quilt! Turn to pages 29–35 for instructions on basting, quilting, and binding. This table runner requires about 190" of binding to finish its edges.

> Chain Reaction Table Runner pattern.

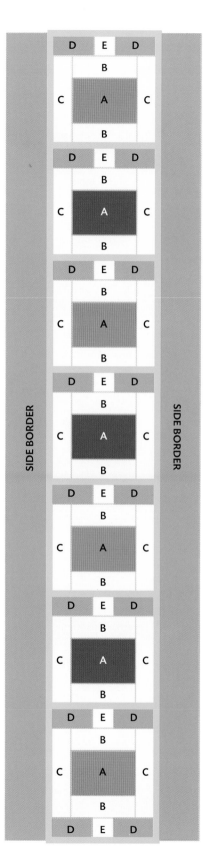

> Piece the blocks

BLOCK 1

Strip

Housetop

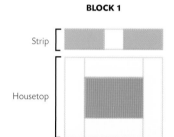

Step 1

Step 2

Step 3

Step 4

SIDE BORDER

SIDE BORDER

> Chain Reaction Table Runner blocks.

link 'em up place mats

While I can't promise that colorful place mats will get your kids to eat their broccoli, they are an easy and affordable way to add a kick of your fave color du jour to your table setting! True, your dining room might be made up of neutrals, but your place mats can show off the color-loving seamster you are. Put color psychology to work by choosing appetite-inspiring solids, like orange or red, to set off the graphic prints inside these bold chain frames. These place mats are designed to coordinate with the Chain Reaction Table Runner (page 112), so make sure you have enough fabric to mix across the projects if you want to make both.

level of difficulty:
Hey, You're Quilting!

finished size:
19" x 14"

total pieces:
84 for a set of four place mats

what you need:

¼ yard solid orange fabric

¼ yard solid brown fabric

⅓ yard solid or printed cream fabric

¼ yard orange print fabric

¼ yard brown print fabric

¼ yard solid orange binding fabric

¼ yard solid brown binding fabric

1 yard backing fabric

1 yard batting

cutting guide
Includes ¼" seam allowance

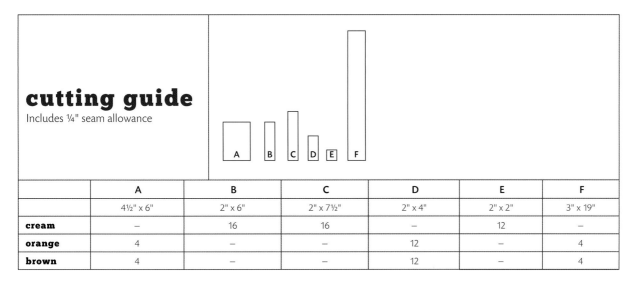

	A	B	C	D	E	F
	4½" x 6"	2" x 6"	2" x 7½"	2" x 4"	2" x 2"	3" x 19"
cream	–	16	16	–	12	–
orange	4	–	–	12	–	4
brown	4	–	–	12	–	4

Cut it out

Using your rotary cutter, ruler, and mat, cut out pieces of your prewashed fabric according to the cutting guide.

Mix it up

Position each piece on your design wall (or some other flat surface) according to the pattern diagram. If necessary, audition different fabrics by cutting out pieces one by one and swapping them in and out until you find a design that you are happy with.

Piece the place mats

Piece the place mats one at a time. Each place mat follows a simple housetop piecing sequence (page 92) in which strips are pieced in turn outward from the center A pieces. Chain-piece the place mat's two housetop configurations simultaneously.

Arrange the pieces for PLACE MAT 1 as they appear in the pattern next to your sewing machine.

1. Select the leftmost A piece and build off it, beginning with the B piece to its left. Pin and sew. Without cutting the thread or lifting the presser foot, move over to the second housetop formation and buddy up the remaining A piece and the B piece to its left. Pin and sew.

    Remove the chain from your sewing machine. Press and cut the threads between the units.

    Reposition the sewn pairs next to your sewing machine according to the pattern diagram.

    On to the next round! Working from left to right, sew the second set of B pieces to the A pieces. Press. Now attach the C pieces to the top and bottom in two more rounds of chain-piecing and pressing.

2. Now focus on the strips next to and between the housetop units. Working from left to right, buddy up the first upper D and E pieces. Pin and sew. Without cutting the thread or lifting the presser foot, move over to the next strip's top D and E pieces, buddy up, and sew. Finally, add the last strip's top D and E pieces to the chain. Press.

    Reposition the sewn pairs next to your sewing machine according to the pattern diagram. On to the next round! Working from left to right, add the remaining D pieces to each strip, sewing in a chain. Press.

3. Now it's time to join your strips and housetop units. Working from the left, sew the first strip to the housetop unit on its right. Next, sew the middle strip to the second housetop unit on its right. Press. Now sew the two joined strip/housetop units together. Next, sew on the last strip on the far right. Press.

4. Sew on the top and bottom F pieces. Press.

Square up your place mat to 19" x 14" by pressing and trimming uneven edges with your rotary cutter.

Repeat the piecing process for the remaining 3 place mats.

Baste, quilt, and bind

Handle these place mats exactly like mini quilts! Turn to pages 29–35 for instructions on basting, quilting, and binding your place mats. Each place mat requires about 75" of binding.

> Link'em Up Place Mats pattern.

Place Mat 1

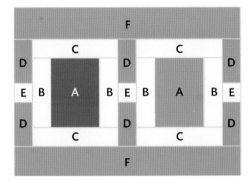

Place Mat 2

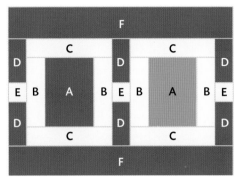

Place Mat 3

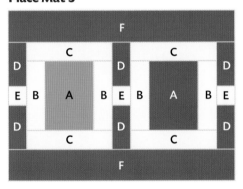

Place Mat 4

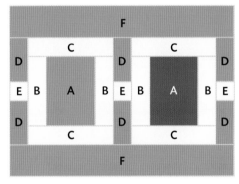

> Piece the place mats.

Step 1

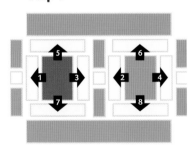

Step 2

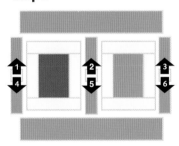

Step 3

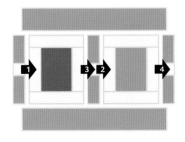

Step 4

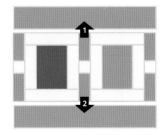

turn up the heat pot holders

Whether it's hot apple pie or seriously spicy three-alarm chili, there isn't anything so hot you can't handle it with this stylish quartet: A layer of heat-resistant batting in your pot-holder sandwich will keep you from getting burned no matter how hot it gets! Placed together in a grid, the plus-sign design continues from piece to piece—just the clever addition your kitchen needs. Speaking of which, pick colors that go with your kitchen (mine happens to look real nice with these brick-reds, mustards, creams, oranges, and complementary blue).

level of difficulty:
Hey, You're Quilting!

finished size:
8½" x 8½"

total pieces:
100 for four pot holders

what you need:
⅛ yard solid blue fabric
⅛ yard solid orange fabric
⅛ yard solid brick-red fabric
⅛ yard cream print fabric
⅛ yard mustard print fabric

⅓ yard solid black backing fabric
¼ yard 45"-wide or ½ yard 22" Insul-Bright heat-resistant batting, available at your local fabric store

¼ yard cotton batting
¼ yard solid black binding fabric

cutting guide
Includes ¼" seam allowance

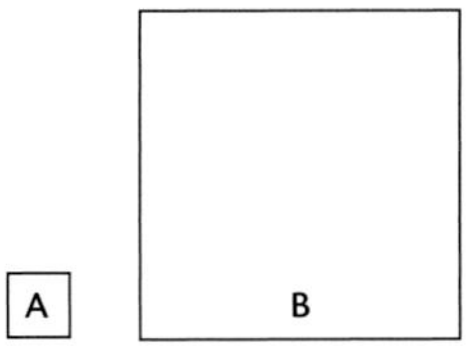

	A	B
	2" x 2"	9" x 9"
blue	19	–
cream	20	–
orange	24	–
mustard	18	–
brick-red	19	–
black	–	4
Insul-Bright batting	–	4
cotton batting	–	4

Cut it out

Using your rotary cutter, ruler, and mat, cut out pieces of your prewashed fabric and batting according to the cutting guide. Set aside the batting and backing fabric.

Mix it up

Position each A piece on your design wall (or some other flat surface) according to the pattern diagram. If necessary, audition different fabrics by cutting out pieces one by one and swapping them in and out until you find a design you are happy with.

Piece the blocks

Tackle the piecing pot holder by pot holder. Arrange the pieces for POT HOLDER 1 as they appear in the pattern next to your sewing machine. Break the block up into 5 rows.

1. From ROW 1, buddy up the leftmost pair of pieces. Pin and sew. Don't cut the thread or lift the presser foot just yet! Now skip to ROW 2, buddying up and sewing the leftmost pair of pieces to the chain. Skip again to ROWS 3, 4, and 5, sewing each row's leftmost two pieces to the chain.

   Remove the chain from your sewing machine. Press and snip the threads between the units.

2. Reposition the sewn pairs next to your sewing machine according to the pattern's POT HOLDER 1 configuration.

   On to the next round! From the upper left, buddy up the joined pair to the neighboring piece on its right. Pin and sew. Don't cut the thread or lift the presser foot just yet! Now skip to the row below it, selecting the leftmost pair and sewing it to the piece to its right. Skip again to ROWS 3, 4, and 5. Press.

   Perform two more rounds of buddying up, skipping rows, and pressing until you have 5 rows.

3. Sew the 5 rows together.

   Square up your pot holder to 8½" x 8½" by pressing and trimming uneven edges with your rotary cutter.

   Repeat piecing process for the remaining 3 pot holders.

Baste and quilt

4. Make a mini quilt sandwich by layering the backing, Insul-Bright batting, cotton batting, and pieced pot holder top.

   Follow the instructions for basting and quilting on pages 30–33.

   Trim off excess backing and batting.

Repeat for the remaining 3 pot holders.

Bind and make hanging loops

Prepare the binding by following the instructions on page 34. Each pot holder will use one selvage-to-selvage strip.

5. Starting on the middle of the left side, snugly wrap the binding around the raw edge of the pot holder and pin. Leaving a loose end of a few inches, sew over the binding ⅛" from the inner edge all the way to the corner of the pot holder. Extend the binding out from the pot holder and continue stitching through it 3" beyond the corner of the pot holder. Backstitch to secure the stitching.

6. Lift the presser foot and cut the thread. Remove the pot holder from your sewing machine. Form a loop with the stitched binding that extends beyond the edge by folding it down and to the left.

   Next, twist it up and back along the top edge of the pot holder. Wrap the binding over the top edge, butting the backstitched end of the binding up against the corner as snugly as possible. Backstitch again, and stitch the binding in place along the top. Finish the binding as described on page 35.

Repeat the binding process for the remaining 3 potholders.

> Turn Up the Heat Pot Holders pattern.

Pot Holder 1 **Pot Holder 2** **Pot Holder 3** **Pot Holder 4**

> Piece the blocks.

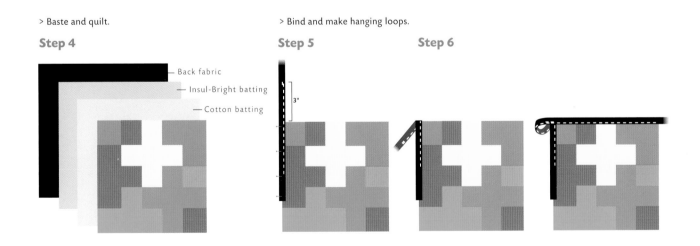

Step 1 **Step 2** **Step 3**

Round 1 Round 2

ROW 1
ROW 2
ROW 3
ROW 4
ROW 5

> Baste and quilt.

Step 4

Back fabric
Insul-Bright batting
Cotton batting

> Bind and make hanging loops.

Step 5 **Step 6**

3"

add some fun apron

If there's cooking going on in my kitchen, it's not being done by me! But this equal-opportunity apron makes it easy for any visiting chef to take top honors. Choose quilting cotton or a more substantial canvas for the body of your apron. I used a solid black fabric that multiplies the sass of the warm and vibrant patterned pocket. Play with different shades of analogous colors in your one-patch design, adding in pops of a bright complementary. Use mostly solids with some quiet prints thrown into the equation. In my apron, a tiny mustard floral adds a pinch of girlie goodness. I won't tell the boys if you won't.

level of difficulty:
Hey, You're Quilting!

finished size:
23" x 26"

total pieces:
36 plus apron body and ties

what you need:
⅛ yard solid blue fabric
⅛ yard solid orange fabric
⅛ yard solid brick red fabric
⅛ yard cream print fabric
⅛ yard mustard print fabric
1 yard solid black quilting
   cotton or canvas

⅓ yard mid-weight non-fusible
   interfacing, available at
   your local fabric mega store

cutting guide
Includes ¼" seam allowance

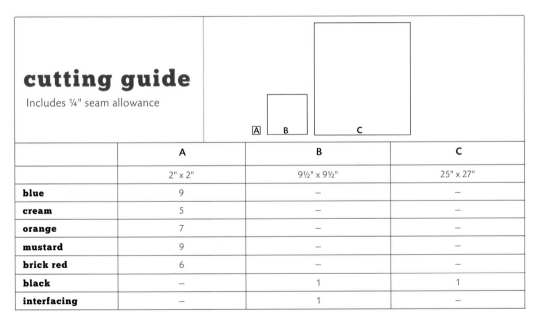

	A	B	C
	2" x 2"	9½" x 9½"	25" x 27"
blue	9	–	–
cream	5	–	–
orange	7	–	–
mustard	9	–	–
brick red	6	–	–
black	–	1	1
interfacing	–	1	–

Cut it out

Using your rotary cutter, ruler, and mat, cut out pieces of your prewashed fabric and interfacing according to the cutting guide. Set aside the black fabric and interfacing.

Mix it up

Position each A piece on your design wall (or some other flat surface) according to the pattern diagram. If necessary, audition different fabrics by cutting out pieces one by one and swapping them in and out until you find a design you are happy with.

Piece the block

Arrange the pieces for the pocket as they appear in the patern next to your sewing machine. Break the block up into 6 rows.

1. From ROW 1, buddy up the leftmost pair of pieces. Pin and sew. Don't cut the thread or lift the presser foot just yet! Now skip to ROW 2, buddying up and sewing the leftmost pair of pieces to the chain. Skip again to the ROWS 3, 4, 5, and 6, sewing each row's leftmost two pieces to the chain.

   Remove the chain from your sewing machine. Press and snip the threads between the pairs.

2. Reposition the sewn pairs next to your sewing machine according to the pattern's configuration. On to the next round! From the upper left, buddy up the joined pair to the neighboring piece on its right. Pin and sew. Don't cut the thread or lift the presser foot just yet! Now skip to the row below it, selecting the leftmost pair and sewing it to the piece to its right. Skip again to ROWS 3, 4, 5, and 6. Press.

> Piece the block.

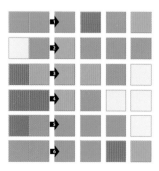

Step 1

Round 1

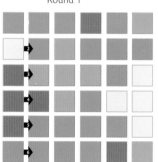

Step 2

Round 2

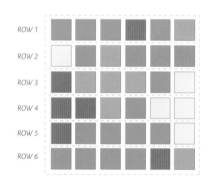

Step 3

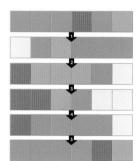

Perform three more rounds of buddying up, chain-piecing, skipping rows, and pressing until you have 6 rows.

3. Sew the 6 rows together.

Square up your pocket to 9½" x 9½" by pressing and trimming uneven edges with your rotary cutter.

Make the pocket

4. Position the 9½" x 9 ½" pieces of black lining fabric and interfacing on top of each other, wrong sides together. Sew around the perimeter, ⅛" from the edge. With the interfacing side up, place the black lining on top of the right side of the pocket front. Align the edges and pin in place.

5. Stitch around the perimeter of the square through all the layers with a ¼" seam allowance, pivoting at each corner. Leave a 2" opening at the center bottom and secure the stitches. Press flat and trim the corners.

Turn the pocket right side out through the opening, gently pushing out the corners into points with your finger. Fold in the seam allowance at the 2" opening. Press flat and set aside.

> Make the pocket.

Step 4

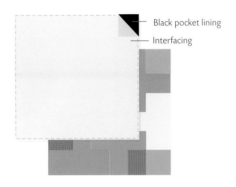

Black pocket lining

Interfacing

Step 5

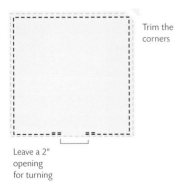

Trim the corners

Leave a 2" opening for turning

> Add Some Fun Apron pattern.

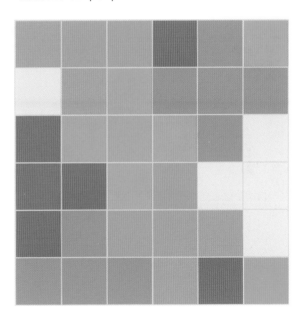

Make the apron

6. On both long sides of your 25" x 27" piece of black fabric, double-turn and pin a ½" hem. Along the bottom, double-turn and pin a ½" hem. Stitch ⅛" from the inside edge of the hem, sewing in a U shape by pivoting at the corners. Secure the stitches.

   For the apron strings, make a 100" length of binding from the black fabric using a tape maker, following the instructions on page 34. For finished ends on the apron string, unfold the ends and fold in ½" of the end. Press. Fold the binding back into place lengthwise and press.

7. Center the 100" strip over the top of the apron, enclosing its top raw edge inside the binding strip. Pin in place. Starting at one end of the apron string, stitch ⅛" from the inside edge of the string, moving from one end to the other—over the apron centered in the middle. Secure the stitches.

   Add the pocket by centering it on the apron's front about 5" from the top edge. Pin in place. Topstitch close to the edge of the pocket, carefully backstitching at the top corners for extra reinforcement.

> Make the apron.

Simply charming

The Add Some Fun Apron and the Turn Up the Heat Pot Holders (page 120), are made from a simple one-patch pattern that gets its lively plus-sign design from clever color placement. But another option is taking these one-patch squares and using a different fabric for every single piece—without duplication. This is the objective of "charm quilts," whose hundreds, even thousands, of fabric pieces are completely unique. Most charm quilts employ a simple one-patch construction, taking a geometric shape, like a square or a triangle, and repeating it over the entire quilt. In the nineteenth century, charm quilts were often referred to as "beggar's" quilts because their makers would continually beg for scraps from family and friends to add to their fabric arsenals. Nowadays, the Internet has provided a way for clever quilters to swap fabrics and maximize the variety within their charming one-patch creations.

Step 6

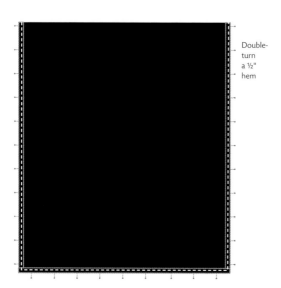

Double-turn a ½" hem

Step 7

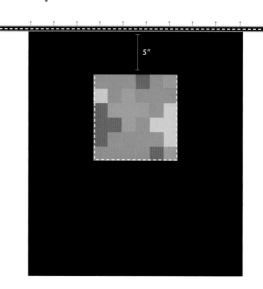

5"

salvaged salutations

No respectable scrap hoarder should ever suffer the indignity of giving a store-bought greeting card. Salvaged Salutations are quick, easy, and all-purpose—yet feel incredibly textured and personal. Forget straight pieces and clean edges; nothing says "You're special" like an off-kilter and unique one-off design. And nothing accompanies a "Thank you" better than a card with one attention-grabbing print surrounded by solids and quieter prints that allow your leading scrap to shine. I prefer utilitarian white thread for the quilting, but experiment with different colors, bearing in mind that your stitching will also be on display inside the card.

level of difficulty:
Straight-Up Sewing

finished size:
4¼" x 5½"

what you need:
4 to 6 fabric scraps in a mix
    of solids and patterns, in
    strips and squares
4¼" x 5½" blank folded
    card—or any size to suit
    your needs
A glue stick
Scissors and pinking shears

Cut it out

Raid your scrap heap for a mix of 4 to 6 strips and squares—enough to cover the front surface of your card. The scraps should extend past the edges of the card about ¼" to ½".

Mix it up

1. Starting with the largest scrap, position it on the card's front with the card open flat. Build upon the first piece by arranging the remaining strips and squares on top of or around it, keeping your pieces in a straight 90-degree composition. Loosely trim scraps to fit as necessary, using pinking shears for some of the edges. Let the scraps hang off the card's edge.

2. When you are satisfied with the card's composition, slide the fabric off the card, being careful to maintain the composition. Select the bottom-most fabric scrap and position it on the front of the card, using a bit of glue from the glue stick on the card to temporarily hold the fabric in place. (A little glue won't gum up your machine's needle, but use sparingly.) Reposition the remaining scraps, securing each piece with a tiny bit of glue.

Sew the scraps

3. Bring your card to your sewing machine for "quilting." Sewing through the fabric and the card, add edge-to-edge lines or concentric squares in any design you choose. Where stitching isn't overlapped by other stitching, backstitch at both ends to lock the thread in place. Snip the thread ends.

4. Fold the card closed, turn it wrong side up, and use your ruler and rotary cutter to trim off the excess fabric around the edge

[Tip] *Replace your machine's needle before you move on to a new sewing project. Card stock can dull a needle's sharpness.*

Taming tiny scraps

No matter what the occasion, I am constantly stitching up Salvaged Salutations—which requires me to have plenty of scraps at the ready. If you never want to show up empty-handed to a birthday or anniversary party, maintain a clear plastic bin for scraps that are oddly shaped or too small to be used in a quilt or larger project. Not only will this be your go-to bin for card construction, you'll find a surprising number of crafty uses for these scraps. The point of keeping scraps is to use them, not hoard them!

> Mix it up.

Step 1

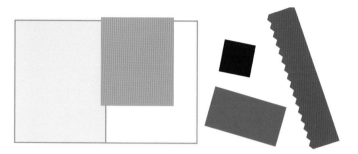

Step 2

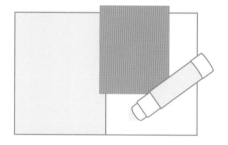

> Sew the scraps.

Step 3

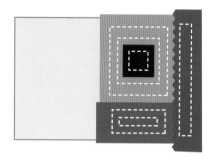

Step 4

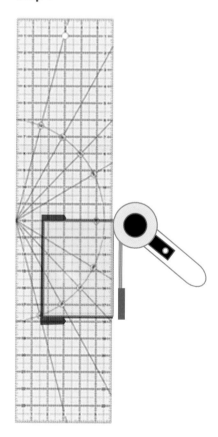

gridlock grocery getter

Loaf of bread, half gallon of orange juice, a bunch of bananas? This grocery getter can carry it all! Up your urban chic as you walk to the market with this enviable tote. You'll look so stylish, no one will mind that you forgot the soy milk! Black, off-white, and multicolored all over, this design gives you permission to raid your fabric stash for the solids you adore. A peek of pink, a sprout of green, a blink of blue—even tiny patches can have big impact with this highly graphic and scrap-friendly design. Pick your favorite fabric for a punchy lining that'll keep you smiling while filling 'er up.

level of difficulty:
Hey, You're Quilting!

finished size:
18½" x 18½" x 5

total pieces:
163 plus 4 border strips

what you need:
⅔ yard solid black fabric
¼ yard solid off-white fabric
⅛ yard assorted solids
1 yard solid blue lining fabric
20" x 20" piece of batting

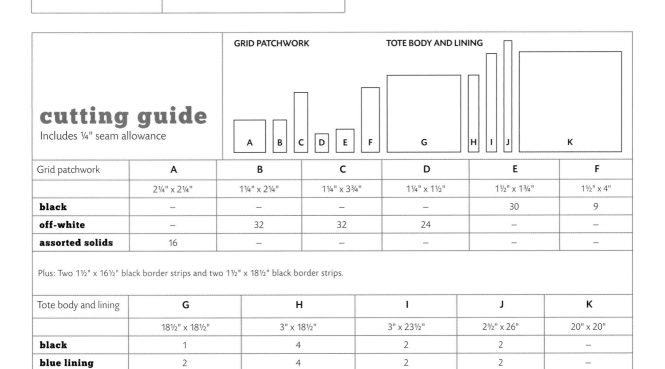

cutting guide
Includes ¼" seam allowance

GRID PATCHWORK — A B C D E F

TOTE BODY AND LINING — G H I J K

Grid patchwork	A	B	C	D	E	F
	2¼" x 2¼"	1¼" x 2¼"	1¼" x 3¾"	1¼" x 1½"	1½" x 1¾"	1½" x 4"
black	–	–	–	–	30	9
off-white	–	32	32	24	–	–
assorted solids	16	–	–	–	–	–

Plus: Two 1½" x 16½" black border strips and two 1½" x 18½" black border strips.

Tote body and lining	G	H	I	J	K
	18½" x 18½"	3" x 18½"	3" x 23½"	2½" x 26"	20" x 20"
black	1	4	2	2	–
blue lining	2	4	2	2	–
batting	–	–	–	–	1

Cut it out

Using your rotary cutter, ruler, and mat, cut out pieces of your prewashed solid fabric according to the cutting guide. Set aside the pieces for the bag's body and lining.

Mix it up

Position each piece of the tote's front grid on your design wall (or some other flat surface) according to the pattern diagram. Audition different solid fabric A pieces until you find a design that you are happy with.

Piece the grid patchwork

The Gridlock Grocery Getter's front grid design is made up of multipiece strips and simple housetop blocks (page 92). First, chain-piece the grid's 16 A-B-B-C-C housetop configurations. Once you complete these squares, chain-piece the horizontal E-D-E strips, followed by the three multipiece vertical strips. Then bring it all together!

1. Working from left to right and top to bottom, select the upper-left A piece. Buddy it up with a B piece to its left. Pin and sew. Without cutting the thread or lifting the presser foot, move over to the next housetop formation. Buddy up the A piece and the B piece to its left. Pin and sew. Continue to chain-piece the remaining A pieces to the B pieces on their left.

    Remove the chain from your sewing machine. Press and cut the threads between the units.

    Reposition the sewn pairs next to your sewing machine according to the pattern diagram. Continue chain-piecing the 16 housetop configurations simultaneously, piecing strips in turn outward from the center A pieces. First add on the remaining B pieces, then attach the C pieces—the tops and then the bottoms—pressing after each set of pieces is sewn.

2. Next focus on the 3-piece strips that run horizontally between the housetop blocks. Chain-piece these 12 E-D-E units. Working from left to right and top to bottom, select the upper-leftmost E piece. Buddy it up with

a D piece to its right. Pin and sew. Without cutting the thread or lifting the presser foot, move over to the next E-D-E strip. Buddy up the first E piece with the D piece to its right. Pin and sew. Continue to chain-piece the remaining first E pieces to the D pieces on their right.

Remove the chain from your sewing machine. Press and cut the threads between the units.

Reposition the sewn pairs next to your sewing machine according to the pattern diagram. Continue chain-piecing the 12 E-D-E units, completing each strip with the E pieces to the right.

3. Next, focus on the 3 multi pieced vertical strips between the housetop blocks. From the first strip on the left, buddy up the top E and D pieces. Pin and sew. Next buddy up the F and D pair directly below it, sewing it onto the chain. Continue moving from top to bottom, buddying up all available pairs and chain-piecing.

    Remove the chain from your sewing machine. Press and snip the threads between the pairs.

    Reposition the sewn pairs next to your sewing machine according to the pattern. Buddy up the top 2 joined pairs. Pin and sew. Next buddy up the joined pairs directly below it, sewing it onto the chain, joining pairs until you have a completed strip. Press. Repeat this process for the remaining 2 vertical strips.

Sew the blocks

4. Chain-sew the housetop blocks to the E-D-E strips, making 4 columns. Remove the chain from your sewing machine. Press and cut the threads between the units.

5. Next, join the 4 columns to the vertical strips in between them. Carefully pin and sew. Sew the 4 columns of patchwork together.

Sew a 1½" x 16½" black border strip to each side. Next, sew a 1½" x 18½" black border strip to the top and bottom.

Square up your grid patchwork by pressing it to 18½" x 18½" and trimming uneven edges with your rotary cutter.

> Gridlock Grocery Getter pattern.

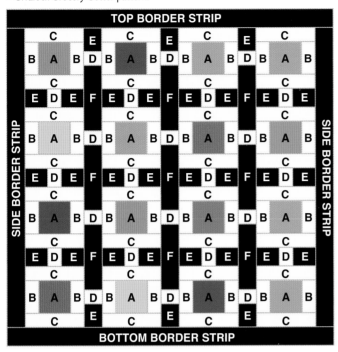

> Piece the grid patchwork.

Step 1

Housetop Block

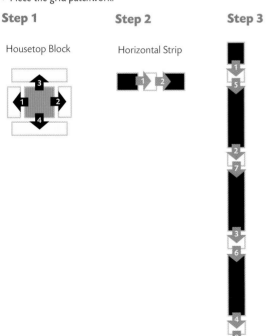

Step 2

Horizontal Strip

Step 3

> Sew the blocks.

Step 4

Step 5

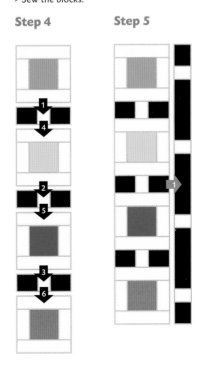

Quilt the grid design

Place the grid patchwork atop the batting. Add diagonal quilting lines—no backing required! Turn to pages 30–33 for instructions on basting and quilting the two layers.

Construct the outside of the tote

6. Build the front of the tote. Sew the black H pieces to the sides of the quilted grid front. Press the seam away from the H piece and topstitch over the seam allowance. Add the I piece along the bottom. Press the seam away from the I piece and topstitch over the seam allowance.

   Repeat for the back of the tote, using the 18½" x 18½" black G piece instead of the patchwork grid.

7. With right sides together, pin the front and back, stitching the sides (the H pieces) and bottom (the I pieces) of the bag. Press flat.

8. Using your hands, shape the 4 sides and bottom of the bag. Fold the lower side corners of the bag flat, forming a triangle from the end of the bottom pieces. Stitch along the seam across corners to make a box bottom. Press the triangle.

   Repeat steps 6–8 with the blue lining pieces to make the tote's lining, using G lining pieces.

> Construct the outside of the tote.

Step 6

Press seams toward center

Topstitch over seam allowance

H   H   H   G   H

I   I

Step 7

Step 8

Stitch across corners

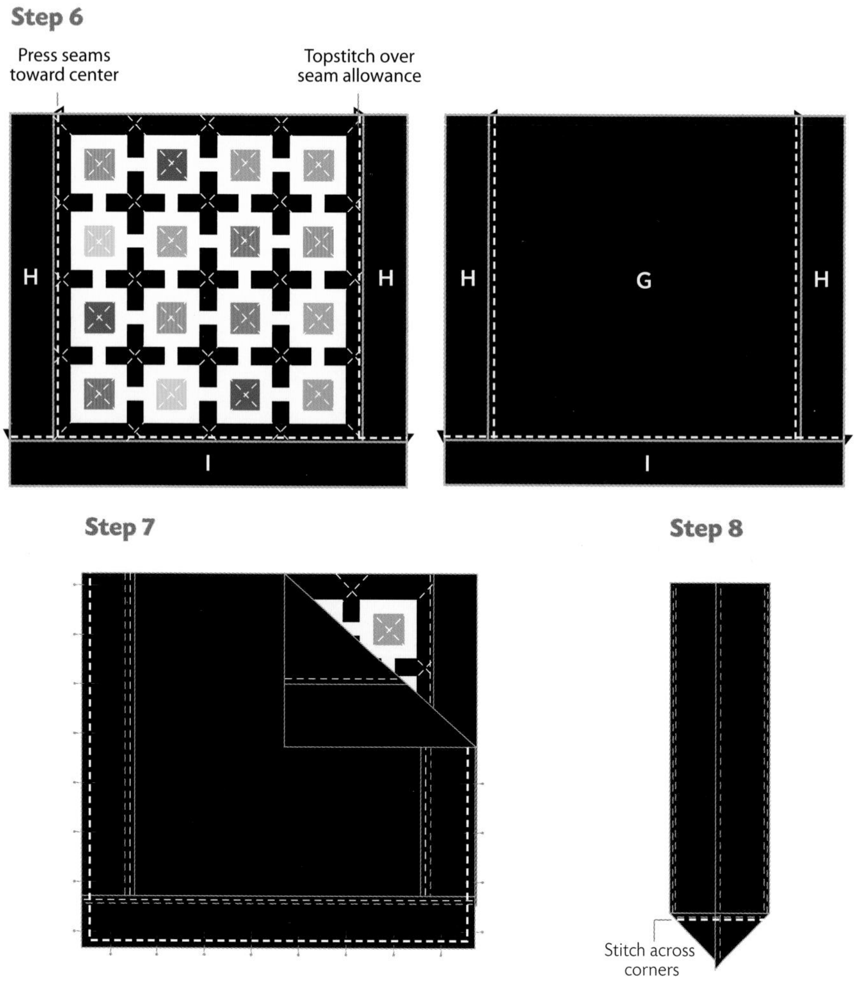

Make the straps

9. With right sides together, pin a black J strip on top of a blue J strip. Stitch along both long sides using a ¼" seam allowance. Press flat.

10. Gently turn the strap inside out. Press flat. Topstitch both long edges of the strap.

    Repeat the process of making the straps with the remaining J strips for the second strap.

Bring all pieces together

11. With right sides together, place the lining bag into the outer bag. Pin the straps in place about 4½" in from the sides, facing down with ends extending ½" beyond the edge of tote. Stitch around the top edges of the lining and outer bag with a ¼" seam allowance, leaving a 5" opening for turning. Backstitch at the stop and start.

12. Turn the bag right side out through the opening. Make sure that the triangles you made in step 8 rest along the bottom of the bag. Topstitch around the top of the bag. Press flat.

> Make the straps.

Steps 9 and 10

Turn inside-out

Topstitch both edges of strap

> Bring all pieces together.

Step 11

Stitch around top leaving an opening to turn

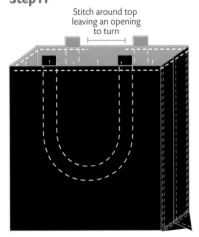

Step 12

Turn and topstitch around top

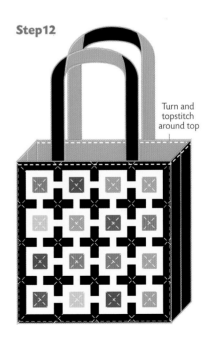

pokey the playmat

Slow down for some playtime with Pokey the laid-back snail. This modern mollusk is unworried and unhurried, carrying everything he needs in a deluxe log cabin design on his back. Choose a warm and welcoming solid, like muted yellow, to create an inviting space. Alternate solids with prints and dark with light values around Pokey's log cabin formation. Pick embroidery floss in a dark, warm color to give Pokey's face stand-out features. A high-loft polyester batting will give extra fluff and padding to the playmat when it's placed on a floor.

level of difficulty:
Hey, You're Quilting!

finished size:
36" x 36"

total pieces:
24 plus 2 border strips

what you need:

1 yard solid yellow fabric

¼ yard total solid blue fabric in 3 shades

¼ yard solid brown fabric

¼ yard solid pink fabric

¼ yard assorted prints in brown, blue, and pink

⅓ yard solid yellow binding fabric

1¼ yards backing fabric

Crib-size batting

Quilt pencil

Embroidery floss and needle

cutting guide
Includes ¼" seam allowance

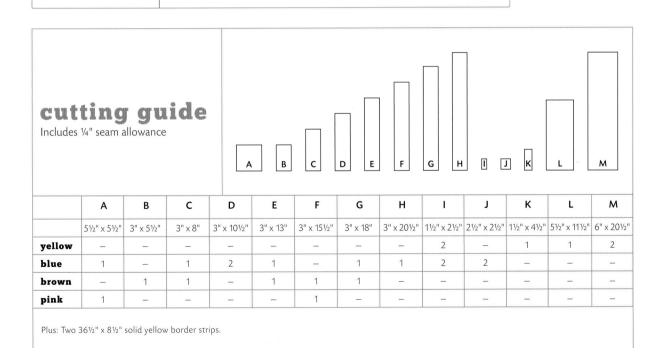

	A	B	C	D	E	F	G	H	I	J	K	L	M
	5½" x 5½"	3" x 5½"	3" x 8"	3" x 10½"	3" x 13"	3" x 15½"	3" x 18"	3" x 20½"	1½" x 2½"	2½" x 2½"	1½" x 4½"	5½" x 11½"	6" x 20½"
yellow	–	–	–	–	–	–	–	–	2	–	1	1	2
blue	1	–	1	2	1	–	1	1	2	2	–	–	–
brown	–	1	1	–	1	1	1	–	–	–	–	–	–
pink	1	–	–	–	–	1	–	–	–	–	–	–	–

Plus: Two 36½" x 8½" solid yellow border strips.

Cut it out

Using your rotary cutter, ruler, and mat, cut out pieces of your prewashed solid fabric according to the cutting guide.

Mix it up

Position each piece on your design wall according to the pattern diagram. Using the Scraphazard Quilt Design technique described on page 20, replace several solid fabric pieces with print pieces in the corresponding color. Audition a mix of print fabrics by cutting out pieces one by one and swapping them in and out until you've reached a lively balance of plain and patterned. Take your time and enjoy this process!

Stitch on Pokey's face

Before you piece the playmat top, stitch the snail's face onto the A piece. First, freehand an eye and mouth with a quilt pencil. Using 6 stands of embroidery floss and an embroidery needle, sew a simple running stitch to create the snail's features, stitching in a spiral to make the eye.

Start and stop with a knot on the wrong side. Press on the wrong side of the face.

Piece the blocks

Pokey just has two simple blocks to piece! BLOCK 1 uses an easy Block Off and Buddy Up strategy (page 26), while BLOCK 2 follows a basic log cabin piecing sequence (page 89), where strips are pieced in turn outward from a center square.

1. Starting with BLOCK 1, arrange the pieces as they appear in the pattern next to your sewing machine. First, let's focus on the antennae. Buddy up the two pairs of I pieces. Pin, sew, and press. Next, sew each pair of I pieces to the J pieces above them. Press. Working from left to right, sew the first antennae unit to the K piece. Next, sew on the second antennae unit. Press. Next, sew the antennae to the A piece below, and then to the L piece above. Press. Finally, sew on the M piece on the left of the unit.

> Piece the blocks.

Step 1

BLOCK 1

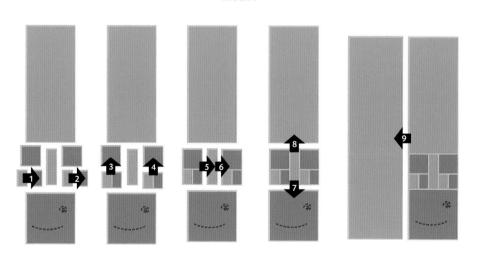

> Pokey the Playmat pattern.

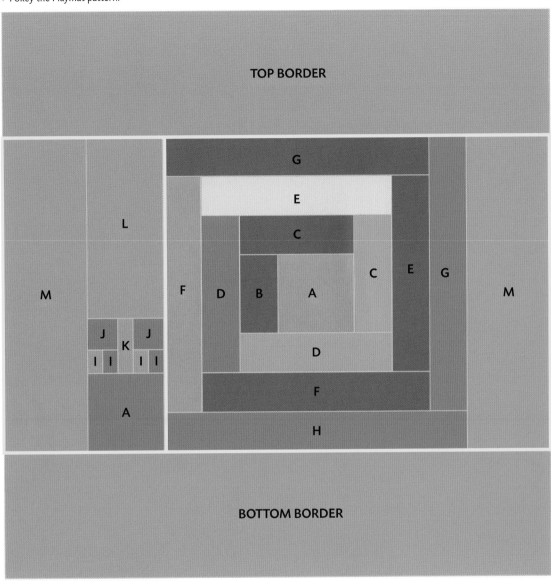

> Pokey the Playmat blocks.

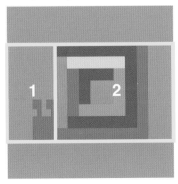

2. On to BLOCK 2! Arrange the pieces as they appear in the pattern next to your sewing machine. Select the A piece in the center and start building off it, beginning with the B piece. Pin, sew, and press. Next, sew on the adjacent C piece. Continue adding strips one side at a time according to the illustration, pressing each seam as you go.

Sew the blocks

Now that you have 2 blocks, it's time to sew them together. Make sure each block is thoroughly pressed. Lay BLOCK 1 on top of BLOCK 2 with right sides together. Secure the 2 blocks with pins. Sew and then press.

Add borders

Add the border strips. With right sides together, pin one of the 36½" x 8½" yellow border strips to the top and the other to the bottom of the snail. Sew and press the seams toward the border.

Finish your playmat

Hang your finished playmat top on your design wall. Stand back and admire it. Way to go! Turn to pages 29–35 for instructions on basting, quilting, and binding your playmat.

A shower of fabrics

Make a Pokey that's extra special for a mother-to-be. At her baby shower, request that each attendee bring a piece of fabric—from her fabric stash, an old cotton shirt, or old baby clothing—that you can work into your playmat. Establish a fabric theme, like nursery prints, blues or pinks, or primary colors. A lively assortment of fabric contributions will make this cute-as-a-bug project even more sweet and meaningful.

Step 2

BLOCK 2

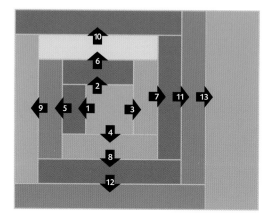

i'm a wiener! baby quilt

It has to be said: This quilt's gone to the dogs. The wiener dogs, that is! This nonstandard dachshund's stacked coins design (page 67) gets its uncommon pedigree from the fabric scraps you choose. A yellow dog? Sure. Pink? Of course! Get out your personality-packed, high-contrast prints, because this dog is designed to handle even the most mischievous of scraps. A complementary-colored backdrop will make your dog jump off the quilt—since my doggy was warm brown, this blue created the pop that won "best in show."

level of difficulty:	what you need:		
Hey, You're Quilting!	1 yard solid blue fabric	1/3 yard assorted prints in	2 yards backing fabric
	3/4 yard total solid brown	shades of brown	Crib-size batting
finished size:	fabric in 3 different	1/8 yard solid black fabric	
40¼" x 40¼"	shades	½ yard solid blue binding	
		fabric	
total pieces:			
90 plus 2 border strips			

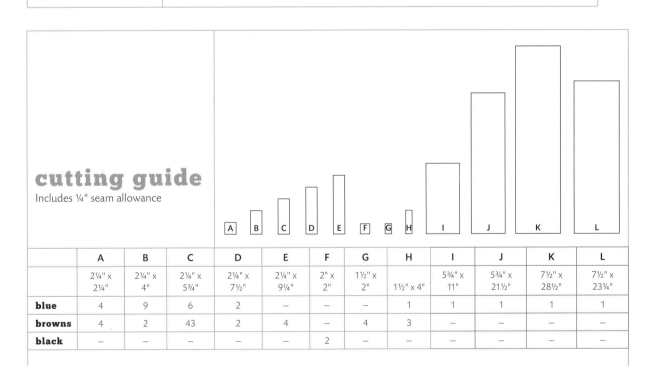

cutting guide
Includes ¼" seam allowance

	A	B	C	D	E	F	G	H	I	J	K	L
	2¼" x 2¼"	2¼" x 4"	2¼" x 5¾"	2¼" x 7½"	2¼" x 9¼"	2" x 2"	1½" x 2"	1½" x 4"	5¾" x 11"	5¾" x 21½"	7½" x 28½"	7½" x 23¼"
blue	4	9	6	2	–	–	–	1	1	1	1	1
browns	4	2	43	2	4	–	4	3	–	–	–	–
black	–	–	–	–	–	2	–	–	–	–	–	–

Plus: One 7¼" x 40¾" blue top border strip and one 4¼" x 40¾" blue bottom border strip.
For a bigger I'm a Wiener! Baby Quilt: Add one or more sets of 6½"-wide border strips around the perimeter. Consult the size chart on page 20.

Cut it out

Using your rotary cutter, ruler, and mat, cut out pieces of your prewashed solid fabric according to the cutting guide. Cut out the largest pieces first.

Mix it up

Position each piece on your design wall according to the pattern diagram. Using the Scraphazard Quilt Design technique described on page 20, replace several solid fabric pieces with print pieces in the corresponding color. Audition a mix of print fabrics by cutting out pieces one by one and swapping them in and out until you've reached a lively balance of plain and patterned. Take your time and enjoy this process!

Piece the blocks

The 10 blocks in this quilt are pieced with the simple Block Off and Buddy Up approach described on page 26. They come together in two wags of a tail.

1. Let's jump right into BLOCK 2. Arrange the pieces in order next to your sewing machine. Break the block up into units that square off.

2. Moving left to right, buddy up the two adjoining A pieces. Pin and sew. Without cutting the thread or lifting the presser foot, select 2 C pieces from the middle of the unit, pin and sew the pair together right behind the first.

   Continue to sew the next pairs of C and A pieces in BLOCK 2 to the chain, following the illustration.

Remove the chain from your sewing machine. Press and cut the threads between the units.

3. Reposition the sewn pairs next to your sewing machine according to the pattern diagram's BLOCK 2 configuration. On to the next round! Now buddy up the next set of pairs. Pin and chain-piece. Continue to move across the block, chain-piecing all available pairs. Press.

4. Perform three more rounds of buddying up, chain-piecing and pressing until the block is completed.

   Square up your block by pressing and trimming uneven edges with your rotary cutter. You've got a completed block! Reposition the block on the design wall.

When you are ready, piece the remaining 9 blocks. Break each block up into units that square off. Using the Block Off and Buddy Up strategy, perform several rounds of buddying up, chain-piecing, and pressing until each block is completed.

Sew the blocks

Now that you have 10 blocks, it's time to sew them into one quilt top. Make sure each block is thoroughly pressed. Starting with BLOCK 2, position it on top of BLOCK 3 with right sides together. Carefully match the seam intersection. Secure the two blocks with pins. Sew and then press. Next, sew BLOCK 4 to BLOCK 3.

> Piece the blocks.

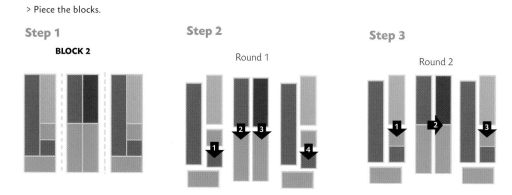

Step 1

BLOCK 2

Step 2

Round 1

Step 3

Round 2

Move on to the row below the first, sewing BLOCK 6 to 7. Sew BLOCK 8 to 9 and then 10. Join the 3 rows together, and then attach BLOCK 1 to the left side and BLOCK 5 to the right side.

Add borders

With right sides together, pin the 7¼" x 40¾" blue border strip along the top of the quilt. Sew and press the seams toward the border.

Add the 4¼" x 40¾" blue border strip along the bottom of the quilt. Sew and press the seams toward the border.

Finish your quilt

Hang your finished quilt top on your design wall. Stand back and admire it. Way to go! Turn to pages 29–35 for instructions on basting, quilting, and binding your quilt.

> I'm a Wiener! Baby Quilt pattern.

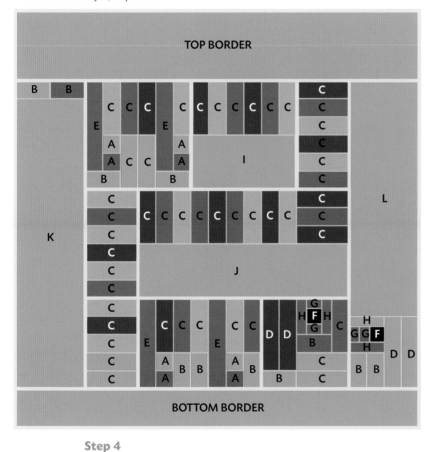

> I'm a Wiener! Baby Quilt blocks.

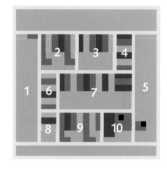

Step 4

Round 3

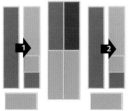

Round 4

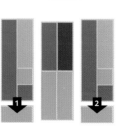

Round 5

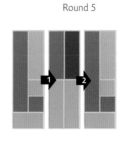

buddy rabbit

Let's say you wanted to build a best friend. You'd probably start by making him or her really smart—like philosophy professor smart. Then, how about some really big ears—ears for listening to troubles and ears for listening to your favorite song on repeat. Lastly, maybe you'd want a little stripey sass to set your friend apart from the crowd. If that's what you'd do, I have a rabbit I'd like you to meet! I used quilt-quality cottons, but a cozy corduroy or a fuzzy flannel would be nice, too. The retro color palette, vintage buttons, and black horn rims give my Buddy a timeless appeal, but use your favorite prints and notions to create a friend all your own.

level of difficulty:
Patchworkin' It

finished size:
7½" x 12½" (not including arms and legs)

total pieces:
33

what you need:
⅓ yard solid blue fabric
⅛ yard solid black fabric
⅛ yard assorted solids and prints in red, orange, yellow, and brown
2 vintage buttons for eyes

Black embroidery floss and needle for mouth
Small bag of polyfill stuffing

cutting guide
Includes ¼" seam allowance

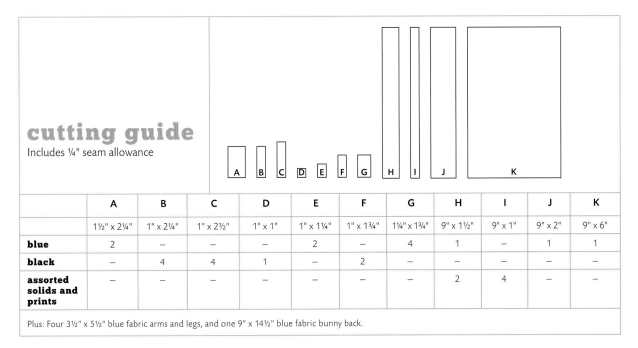

	A	B	C	D	E	F	G	H	I	J	K
	1½" x 2¼"	1" x 2¼"	1" x 2½"	1" x 1"	1" x 1¼"	1" x 1¾"	1¼" x 1¾"	9" x 1½"	9" x 1"	9" x 2"	9" x 6"
blue	2	–	–	–	2	–	4	1	–	1	1
black	–	4	4	1	–	2	–	–	–	–	–
assorted solids and prints	–	–	–	–	–	–	–	2	4	–	–

Plus: Four 3½" x 5½" blue fabric arms and legs, and one 9" x 14½" blue fabric bunny back.

Cut it out

Using your rotary cutter, ruler, and mat, cut out pieces of your prewashed solid fabric according to the cutting guide. Set aside the pieces for the bunny's arms, legs, and back.

Mix it up

Position each piece on your design wall (or some other flat surface) according to the pattern diagram. Audition different fabrics for the bunny's shirt until you find a design that you are happy with.

Piece the patchwork front

Arrange the pieces for the bunny's front as they appear in the pattern next to your sewing machine. Divide the bunny up into 3 sections: the top K piece, the eyeglasses, and the shirt strips.

1. Starting with the eyeglasses, break the block apart and buddy up pieces for chain-piecing. Working from left to right, select the top-leftmost G piece. Pin and sew it to the F piece below it. Without cutting the thread or lifting the presser foot, move to the right and select the A piece and the B piece above it. Pin and sew. Continue to chain-piece the remaining available pairs.

   Remove the chain from your sewing machine. Press and cut the threads between the units.

   Reposition the pairs in order next to your sewing machine. Buddy up new pairs for chain-piecing. Continue with two more rounds of buddying up and chain-piecing until the eyeglasses are complete.

2. Next, focus on the section of strips that make up the bunny's body. Buddy up pieces for chain-piecing. Working from top to bottom, select the top H piece. Pin and sew it to the I piece below it. Without cutting the thread or lifting the presser foot, move to the pair below it. Pin and sew. Continue to chain-piece the remaining available pairs.

> Piece the patchwork front.

Step 1

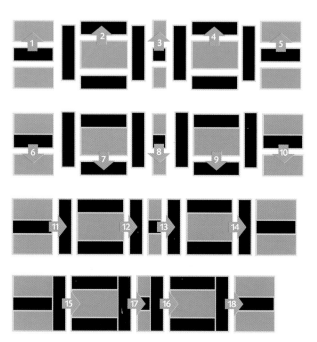

Step 2

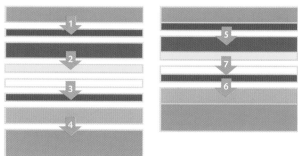

> Buddy Rabbit pattern.

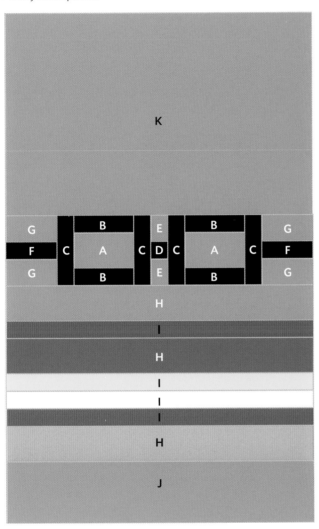

> Buddy Rabbit blocks.

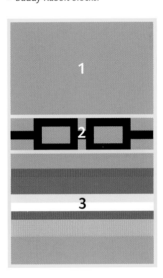

Remove the chain from your sewing machine. Press and cut the threads between the units.

Reposition the pairs in order next to your sewing machine. Buddy up new pairs for chain-piecing. Continue with several more rounds of buddying up and chain-piecing until the striped section is complete.

Sew the 3 sections together.

Make the arms and legs

3. Select the four 3½" x 5½" cuts of blue fabric for the arms and legs. With right sides together, fold each rectangle in half lengthwise. Stitch along the open side and the bottom end. Secure the thread. Trim the corners and press flat. Turn inside out and stuff with polyfill.

Cut out the body

4. Enlarge the Buddy Rabbit body template on page 154 by 200 percent. Cut it out and center on top of the patchwork front. With a quilt pencil, trace around the edge of the cutout. Carefully cut out the patchwork bunny shape with scissors. Also trace the template onto the 9" x 14½" blue fabric bunny back and cut it out.

Add facial features

Now is the best time to stitch on the button eyes and embroider the mouth. For the mouth, freehand a smile with a quilt pencil. Using 6 strands of black embroidery floss and an embroidery needle, stitch a long straight stitch. Start and stop with a knot on the wrong side. Press on the wrong side of the face.

Make a bunny sandwich

5. Pin the arms and legs in place on the right side of the patchwork front, referring to the notches on the rabbit template for suggested placement. Extend the limbs ¼" beyond the body's edge. Using a long stitch on your sewing machine, baste the limbs in place close to the edge.

6. With right sides together, position the bunny back on top of the patchwork front. Carefully align the edges and pin over the pile of arms and legs. Leaving an opening between the bunny's legs, slowly stitch around the perimeter of the body, backstitching at the beginning and the end to secure the stitches. With scissors, trim small, pie-slice shaped notches in the seam allowance around the curves. Press seams flat.

Carefully turn the bunny right side out through the opening. Smooth out curves between your fingers by rolling the seam edges. Press flat. Stuff with polyfill. Insert just enough stuffing to give them shape.

Turn in the seam allowance at the opening. Pin. Hand-stitch the opening closed.

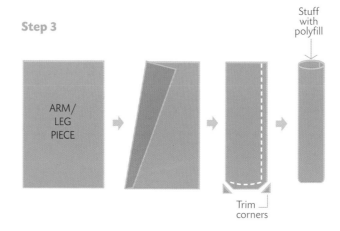

Step 3

ARM/
LEG
PIECE

Trim corners

Stuff with polyfill

Step 4

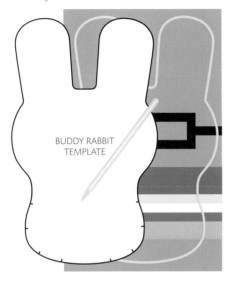

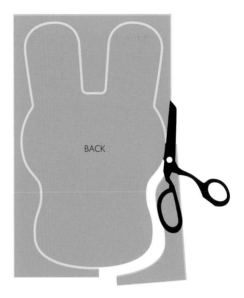

BUDDY RABBIT
TEMPLATE

BACK

Step 5

Step 6

Clip out
notches
around
curves

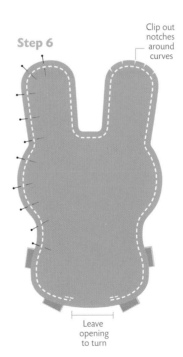

Leave
opening
to turn

templates

Buddy Rabbit Template
Shown at 50%,
enlarge by 200%

Use lines to align multiple
pieces of paper

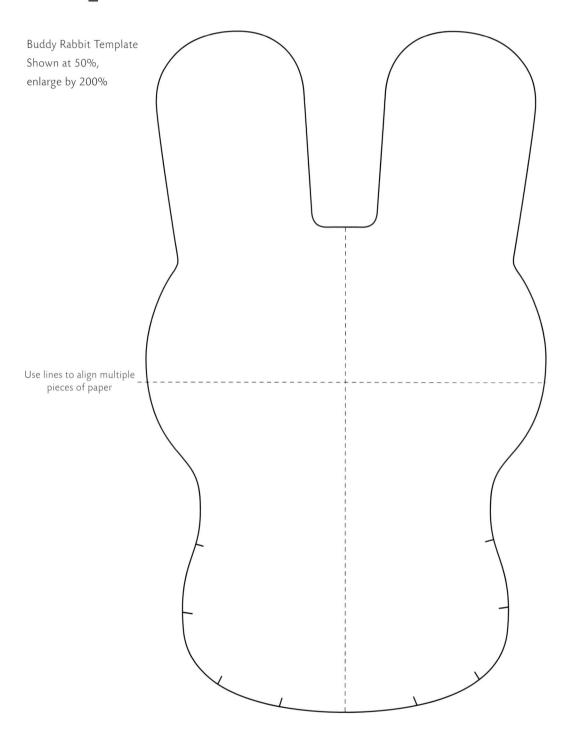

Blockheads Template
Shown at 50%,
enlarge by 200%

Small face

X-small face

glossary

ALL-OVER QUILTING: Stitching that covers the entire quilt without regard for block shapes or patchwork design.

ANALOGOUS COLORS: Colors that sit next to one another on the color wheel.

APPLIQUÉ: When a piece of fabric, usually in a shape, is sewn onto a background fabric with hand or machine stitches. You won't find any of that in this book!

BASTING: Holding two fabrics or layers of a quilt sandwich together temporarily with large hand or machine stitches, or with bent-arm safety pins.

BATTING: The warm middle layer of the quilt sandwich, made of cotton, polyester, cotton/poly, wool, silk, or bamboo. Batting comes in low-, mid-, and high-lofts, or thicknesses.

BIAS: The diagonal grain of a fabric. This is the direction that has the most give or stretch. Never cut on the bias for the straight-sided projects in this book.

BINDING: The narrow fabric strip used to finish the raw edges of a quilt.

BLOCK OFF AND BUDDY UP: The seat-of-your-pants piecing method used for quilts in this book. Blocks gets broken up into units that square off, and within each unit, pieces get paired up, sewn together, and then paired up again.

CHAIN-PIECING (OR QUICK-PIECING, OR CHAIN-SEWING): Sewing pairs of fabric pieces together one after the other without lifting the presser foot or cutting the thread. This saves time and thread.

COMPLEMENTARY COLORS: Pairs of colors that sit opposite one another on the color wheel.

CROSSWISE GRAIN: The threads running perpendicular to the selvage across the width of a fabric. Has a slight stretch.

DOMINANT COLOR: The first color you notice when looking at a quilt because it advances in a design.

EASING: Working in extra fabric where two pieces do not align precisely.

ECHO QUILTING: Stitching multiple lines that follow the outline of patchwork, echoing its shape.

GRAIN: The direction the threads run in a woven fabric.

FABRIC WIDTH: Fabric is manufactured in standard widths, which is the measurement from selvage to selvage.

FAT QUARTER: A uniquely cut ¼ yard piece of fabric that measures 18" x 22".

FILLER PATTERN: Simple all-over quilting design that easily fills large areas of a quilt.

LENGTHWISE GRAIN: The threads running parallel to the selvage in a fabric. It's the strongest grain in your fabric with little stretch.

LONG-ARM QUILTING MACHINE: Big contraption that accommodates large quilts, securing all of the layers tautly in a frame—eliminating the need for basting. Its "long arm" sewing head moves over the stationary quilt top.

MACHINE-BINDING (OR ONE-STEP BINDING): Fast method of binding a quilt that uses a bias tape maker to make folded binding strips that get wrapped over the raw edges of the quilt and sewn on with one pass through a machine.

MACHINE-QUILTING: Using a machine to straight stitch through all three layers of a quilt in a design.

MONOCHROMATIC: Containing or only using one color.

ON-POINT: Quilt blocks or pieces that are positioned on the diagonal.

PATCHWORK: Sewing small pieces of fabric together to create a larger design.

PIECING: The process of sewing together the pieces of a quilt top.

PRESS: A fundamental step in the quilt-making process. To flatten fabric using heat, steam, and pressure.

PRESSER FOOT: The part of a sewing machine that holds the fabric firmly onto the needle plate so the needle can pass through the fabric.

QUILT: Bedcovering comprised of a top, batting, and backing and held together with quilting stitches or ties.

QUILTING: Sewing lines of stitching, usually in a decorative design, to hold the three layers of a quilt together. Quilting can be done by hand or machine, both using a simple running stitch.

QUILT SANDWICH: The three parts of a quilt layered together—the quilt top, batting, and backing.

QUILT TOP: The top patchwork layer of a quilt.

RIGHT SIDE: The printed or public side of fabric.

ROTARY CUTTING: A fast and efficient method of cutting using a sharp, circular blade along the edge of a thick plastic ruler to cut through fabric that has been placed on a special cutting mat.

SCRAPHAZARD: When scrappy and haphazard collide. A charming, random arrangement of prints in a quilt design.

SEAM ALLOWANCE: The area between the edge and the stitching line on two pieces of fabric being stitched together. A ¼" seam allowance is the rule for patchwork and quilting.

SELVAGE: The finished edges of fabric yardage.

resources

Recommended reading from this craft book junkie's quilting and sewing library:

SETTING THE SEAM: The first pressing of the seam as it comes from the sewing machine. This settles the stitches into the fabric and smoothes out puckers before pressing the seam open or to one side.

SQUARING UP A BLOCK: Straightening up a sewn block by pressing to the proper size and trimming uneven edges.

SQUARING UP FABRIC: Straightening one edge of the fabric prior to rotary cutting to ensure straight grain cuts.

STITCH IN THE DITCH: Quilting just next to the seams on the quilt surface to define its shapes.

STRIP-PIECING: A fast piecing method where you cut multiple strips, join them together, and cut into smaller joined units.

VALUE: The degree of lightness or darkness of a color

WRONG SIDE: The side opposite the printed fabric.

YARN-TIED: An alternative to quilting. Yarn is stitched at regular intervals through all three layers of the quilt and knotted on the quilt surface.

Bend-the-Rules Sewing: The Essential Guide to a Whole New Way to Sew by Amy Karol (Potter Craft, 2007)
This book exceeds all legal limits of cute! It's so colorful and sassy, you won't even realize you're learning new terms and techniques.

Denyse Schmidt Quilts: 30 Colorful Quilt and Patchwork Projects by Denyse Schmidt (Chronicle Books, 2005)
All hail to the queen! Denyse Schmidt's graphic sensibility sets the standard in modern quilting.

From Fiber to Fabric: The Essential Guide to Quiltmaking Textiles by Harriet Hargraves (C&T Publishing, 1997)
If you're curious about fabric, this is like getting a PhD in fabricology.

Heirloom Machine Quilting: Comprehensive Guide to Hand-Quilting Effects Using Your Sewing Machine by Harriet Hargraves (C&T Publishing, 2004)
Have dreams of entering the county fair quilt competition? Get this book to take the leap beyond straight-line quilting.

Last-Minute Patchwork & Quilted Gifts by Joelle Hoverson (STC Craft, 2007)
Only got a few hours to make a gift? This irresistible collection of modern quilting and patchwork projects is organized by the amount of time they take to sew.

The Modern Quilt Workshop: Patterns, Techniques, and Designs from the Fun Quilts Studio by Weeks Ringle and Bill Kerr (Quarry Books, 2005)
This really is like a quilt workshop in a book. Such a great investment! Weeks and Bill are like the crafty aunt and uncle you wish you had.

The Quilters Ultimate Visual Guide: From A to Z—Hundreds of Tips and Techniques for Successful Quiltmaking edited by Ellen Pahl (Rodale Press, 1997)

This terrific resource is jam-packed full of expert tips straight from hardcore quilters. Like really hardcore.

Quiltmaker's Color Workshop: FunQuilts' Guide to Understanding Color and Choosing Fabrics by Weeks Ringle and Bill Kerr (Rockport Publishers, 2006)
If you'd like to enlist in color boot camp, this is the book for you.

The Quilts of Gee's Bend: Masterpieces from a Lost Place by Paul Arnett, William Arnett, John Beardsley, and Jane Livingston (Tinwood Books, 2002)
Respect! These quilting geniuses of abstract art will give you a kick in the butt and inspire you to scrappier heights.

The Ultimate Quilting Book: Over 1,000 Inspirational Ideas and Practical Tips by Maggi McCormick Gordon (Collins & Brown, 1999)
This big, fat tome is both a quilt history lesson and a quilting 101, with lots of scrumptious photos of quilts through the ages.

Inspiration for adding embellishments to your quilts:

Bend the Rules with Fabric: Fun Sewing Projects with Stencils, Stamps, Dye, Photo Transfers, Silk Screening, and More by Amy Karol (Potter Craft, 2009)
Approachable and fun, this book is guaranteed to shift your idea machine into high gear.

Printing by Hand: A Modern Guide to Printing with Handmade Stamps, Stencils, and Silk Screens by Lena Corwin (Stewart, Tabori & Chang, 2008)
This gorgeous guide features impeccable step-by-steps on every fabric-printing technique you can think of.

Sublime Stitching: Hundreds of Hip Embroidery Patterns and How-To by Jenny Hart (Chronicle Books, 2006)
If you'd like to add embroidery to your projects, this easy-to-use guide will have you up and stitching in no time.

Subversive Cross Stitch: 33 Designs for Your Surly Side by Julie Jackson (Chronicle Books, 2006)
A perfectly approachable guide to cross stitch, this book will get you thinking about really making a unique mark on your projects.

Sources for fabric & supplies:

Fabric Depot
My mecca for solid fabric and other beautiful basics.
888-896-1478
www.fabricdepot.com

Hancock's of Paducah
Serious quilters be lovin' this joint for all their fabric needs.
800-845-8723
www.hancocks-paducah.com

Nancy's Notions
That's Nancy as in quilting guru Nancy Zieman. Great tips and tools.
800-833-0690
www.nancysnotions.com

Reprodepot Fabric
As their tagline says, a unique selection of fabulous vintage reproduction and retro fabrics.
www.reprodepotfabrics.com

metric conversion chart

Precise measurements are important to quilt-making, and for this reason a direct conversion of the projects in this book from U.S. to metric numbers is less than desirable. These rounded measurements can create imprecision that causes problems across blocks and rows that have lots of pieces. A direct conversion also makes the metric numbers a bit impractical to work with, producing sizes that are not the easiest to cut with a metric ruler. Complicating matters further, the U.S. standard ¼" seam allowance converts to 6.35mm, which is a bit off from the metric standard of 5mm. So, what's a metric-loving quilter to do? Well, for rough metric equivalents that are useful in understanding the following instructions, consult the following chart. But for more accurate measurements to use in cutting out projects, visit www.daretobesquarequilting.com/metric to find project cutting guides that have been recalculated just for my friends outside of the United States.

INCHES TO METRIC						YARDS TO METRIC	
⅛"	3mm	9¼"	23.5cm	28"	71cm		
¼"	6mm	9½"	24cm	28½"	72cm	⅛ yard	12cm
½"	13mm	10"	25.5cm	36"	91cm	¼ yard	23cm
¾"	2cm	10½"	26.5cm	36½"	93cm	⅓ yard	30cm
1"	2.5cm	11"	28cm	40¼"	102cm	⅜ yard	35cm
1¼"	3cm	11½"	29cm	40¾"	103.5cm	½ yard	46cm
1½"	3.8cm	12"	30.5cm	45"	114cm	⅝ yard	57cm
1¾"	4.5cm	12½"	32cm	56½"	143.5cm	⅔ yard	61cm
2"	5cm	13"	33cm	60"	152.5cm	¾ yard	69cm
2¼"	5.5cm	13½"	34.5cm	60½"	154cm	⅞ yard	80cm
2½"	6.5cm	14"	35.5cm	62"	157.5cm	1 yard	91cm
2¾"	7cm	14½"	37cm	62½"	159cm	1¼ yards	1.1m
3"	7.5cm	15½"	39.5cm	63"	160cm	1⅜ yards	1.3m
3⅜"	8.6cm	16½"	42cm	64½"	164cm	1½ yards	1.4m
3½"	9cm	17½"	44.5cm	72"	183cm	1⅝ yards	1.5m
3¾"	9.5cm	18"	45.5cm	72½"	184cm	1¾ yards	1.6m
4"	10cm	18½"	47cm	74"	188cm	2 yards	1.8m
4¼"	11cm	19"	48.5cm	75"	190cm	2⅛ yards	1.9m
4½"	11.5cm	19½"	49.5cm	100"	2.5m	2¼ yards	2m
5"	12.5cm	20"	51cm	190"	4.8m	3 yards	2.7m
5½"	14cm	20½"	52cm			3¼ yards	3m
5¾"	14.5cm	21½"	54.5cm			4 yards	3.7m
6"	15cm	22"	56cm				
6½"	16.5cm	23"	58.5cm				
7"	18cm	23¼"	59cm				
7¼"	18.5cm	23½"	60cm				
7½"	19cm	24½"	62cm				
8"	20.5cm	25"	63.5cm				
8½"	21.5cm	26"	66cm				
9"	23cm	27"	68.5cm				

acknowledgments

TO MY DREAM TEAM:

Margaret Chin, I believe you are actually an angel. Your impeccable piecework saved the day. This book wouldn't exist without your good heart and talented hands.

Alayne Pettyjohn at City Quilting (cityquilting.com), thank you for being a willing adventurer in diagonal quilting on a long-arm machine. Your superb stitching and enthusiasm made these quilts sing.

Kimberlee Iblings, master seamstress and advisor on the small projects, your marvelous sewing assistance and lively chitchat kept my energy high.

Kevin Kosbab, fellow quilter and technical editing guru, you did an amazing job of checking my patterns for accuracy and making my instructions readable and clear.

Jennifer Lévy, thank you for opening up your home to my quilts and photographing them so thoughtfully. Also, thank you Chi Ling Moy for lending your artistic eye to the shots.

Chris Larralde, thank you for the terrific step-by-step photographs. I owe ya, buddy.

Thank you, Rosy Ngo and Thom O'Hearn at Potter Craft for your vision, and Rebecca Behan for seeing this book through the process so handily. You guys are great at what you do.

Thank you, Kate McKean, my agent, for planting the seeds.

TO MY CIRCLE OF TRUST:

Heather Burgess, you got me through this alive. Thank you for your brilliant idea-generating, your impeccable eye, and contagious laughter. You gave me perspective when I was overwhelmed and helped me find the right words. This book is as much yours as it is mine.

Michele McMullen, thank you for your kindness, optimism, and endless supply of empathy. You've been my cheerleader and my unfailing documenter in photos. Thank you for never letting an occasion escape unspecial.

Whitney Stensrud, thank you for your smart opinions on my works-in-progress, your amazing analytical mind and humor, and your even-keeled sensibility. My fellow connoisseur of "single, thirty-something women taking on the world" fiction—someday we'll write our own happily-ever-afters, sister.

Dubba and Squirrel, my faithful feline companions, you were a big part of this process, but sadly, you weren't helpful at all.

TO MY FRIENDS AND SUPPORTERS:

So many friends helped make this book possible, some of you simply by being there: Manny Athens, Brian Biggert, Peter Brandt and Lida Husik, Tina "Pokey" Gregorious, Jane Hudson and Robert Higdon, Scott Jones, Lauren Larralde, Erin Larsen, Jake Lundwall, Chris McMullen, Mike Moon, my Buddhist Kimberly Peterson, Mark Rahner, Randy Tonkin, Mark Tye, Steve Withycombe, Ted Zolyniak, and my Seattle-to-Portland cycling crews—past, present, and future. Also, thanks Dad and Jacklyn.

Thank you, Jesse LeDoux (thepatentpending.com), for letting me turn your amazing Mogwai poster into a quilt.

Thank you to the friends and supporters of Quiltsrÿche: All City Coffee, Kirsten Anderson at Roq La Rue Gallery, Niccole and Abe Brennan, Heather Coats at Quilt or Dye!, Josh Hooten and Michelle Schwegmann at Herbivore, Shane Mehling, my graphics family at *The Seattle Times*, the original stitch'n'bitcher Beth Summanen, and Todd Werny at Space Oddity.

TO MY MOM:

Lastly, thank you, Mom, for ironing a football field of quilt backing and pressing enough binding to go to the moon and back. What would I have done without you to restock my fridge when I was sick and repeatedly shove a wad of twenties into my pocket saying, "I know you need this, kid." You're the best, Ma.

index